DOWN
BUT NOT
OUT

Overcoming Situational Depression

Susan Easton Black

Printed in the United States of America

First Printing, 2019

ISBN 978-0-9995327-4-4

Redstone Media
PO Box 900134
Sandy, Utah 84090-0134

Cover and book design by Daniel Ruesch Design, Inc.

Cover illustration by Julie Rogers.

Black & White illustrations by Jolynn Forman and
Kylie Grace Johnson.

Order copies from Redstonemedia.org

To my readers,
for believing that a Church historian
might know something
about life's challenges

Contents

Introduction

It isn't everyday a Church historian announces, "I'm a psychologist." Hoping to avoid those seeking advice on marital or family problems, I put my training and degrees on the back burner to pursue my passion—Church history and doctrine. I rationalized that there would never be a better life for me than learning and teaching about Joseph Smith and the foundations of the Restoration. And so it was, but it wasn't perfect. I watched from the sidelines as family and friends became less functional as the tentacles of situational depression took hold. Assuring myself that there were better psychologists than me to pick them up, I discounted promptings and pursued my passion with gusto. I ignored urgent calls for help from the emotionally wounded much like a referee who looks the other way when his favorite team needs a win. I did little more than take a casserole or loaf of bread to those whose lives needed so much more.

Perhaps it was the cancer diagnosis or the death of my husband that was my wake up call. Maybe it was the gnawing feeling that I should do more. Whatever the reason I could no longer permit myself to ignore the sufferer of situational depression. Helping the one in a therapy setting at LDS Social Services in Provo, Utah proved rewarding, yet wanting to help more has been my all-consuming thought. It has nothing to do with putting my name up in neon lights as the psychologist with all the answers—the doctor Phil of Mormondom nor does it have anything to do with lining my pockets from those who know too much of heartache. It has everything to do with my desire to share one message: "You may have been knocked down, but you are not out. Situational depression can be overcome."

What do I mean by situation depression? Ask anyone who has lost a loved one, been through a devastating divorce, or any number of life's challenges. Situational depression begins by stopping you in your tracks—taking you out of your normal routine and inhibiting your ability to function normally.

Have you ever wondered why some people glide through life and others hit every bump in the road? Why do some feel only temporarily hopeless and bounce back into life's activities full of energy and creative ideas, ever seeking new avenues for achieving goals while others never rise to the top again? The answer is—you cannot be a passive participant in rising to the top. You can discover the fury of a hurricane by walking against it, not by lying down on the ground. A man who succumbs to the momentary disappointment simply does not know what it would have been like an hour, a week, or a lifetime later if he had faced the disappointment head on. I want to help you navigate when you are thrown off your course—when the very pillars that undergird your happiness are shaken for I know that situational depression can be overcome.

As you read *Down But Not Out*, please know that any mistakes in content are mine. If you find the text an easy read thanks goes to Kathy Gordon, a consummate editor. If you like youthful insights filled with wisdom and candor, research assistants Eliza Allen and Anna Arts deserve the praise. Dennis Lyman, the final word on whether this book would be published, should be cheered for he asked the poignant question, "Who among us has not faced situational depression?" And most of all, heartfelt appreciation is extended to my readers for believing that a Church historian might know something about life's challenges and have the training to help.

CHAPTER ONE

The Situation

My husband suffered from cancer for five years. I was always optimistic that he could beat it. Seven operations, a dozen rounds of chemotherapy, and even more rounds of radiation did not dim my hope. The battle for his life was real but my optimism was just as sure. It wasn't until his last breath that my hope extinguished and my loss became irretrievable.

Most women in my situation would have made funeral arrangements months, if not years, in advance. They would have picked out a casket and selected a favorite flower arrangement but not me. The mortician's arrival at my home with a glossy brochure featuring his popular caskets was unwanted and unsolicited. I was not prepared to make a decision and asked him to leave.

Knowing that a decision needed to be forthcoming, a family member agreed to help and said, "Dad wanted to be buried in a pine box. I'll find just the right one." I was grateful for her assistance, and the find of a Costco casket online until another family member stormed through the front door exclaiming, "My father will never be buried in a Costco casket. Dad deserves the best." Wanting to avoid a family squabble, I agreed to choose a suitable casket. After all, I wanted the best for the love of my life and nothing but the best would do.

I telephoned the mortuary and to my chagrin they sent the same mortician wearing the same dark suit and sporting the same gloomy demeanor to my home. What I remember is that the mortician talked endlessly about caskets, assuring me that I was doing right by my loved one. But I had no such feeling when I opened the bill tucked between the sympathy cards that had arrived that morning in the mail.

With no one standing nearby to comfort me, I discovered that I had spent over $18,000 for the casket, hearse, and other funeral arrangements. Perhaps my tears had covered the bottom line of the contract the day the mortician paid his visit, but not anymore. I glanced through the itemized statement to see if there had been a mistake. Sure enough, there was a mistake. I had paid fifty dollars for the mortician to comb my husband's hair. "That's impossible!" I said aloud. "He was bald for over two decades. It wasn't the chemotherapy that took his hair, it was life."

I got dressed in my own black attire, drove to the mortuary, and marched into the mortician's office to lodge a formal complaint. "My bill is incorrect," I said to the receptionist. Not wanting to confront my wrath, she directed me to the office of the owner of the mortuary. From his stuffed chair and with a large desk as a buffer between us, he assured me that we had a contract and that if he deleted the fifty dollars from my bill, I would no longer have his package deal of $18,000 and would owe him more money.

I left the mortuary irritated but confident that I would never use their service again or recommend their pushy salesman to any other grieving widow. I was anxious to retreat to the walls of my own home where I could more clearly sort out the new difficulties of my life. At home I carefully read the contract again. What stood out this time was that I had paid for three counseling sessions with a grief counselor.

Knowing that I was filled with grief and would need help to move forward in this phase of my life, I telephoned the mortuary and got the name and number of the counselor. I then phoned the counselor and made an appointment. She agreed to see me the following Tuesday at 7:00 pm.

As the time of my appointment neared I put on my black skirt and sweater and tried to look as good as any woman could who had just lost her husband and was in her sixties. When I arrived at the counselor's office, I was surprised that she was wearing casual clothes, which obviously dates me. I was directed to sit in a chair and she pulled up another chair to be close to me. She began the session by informing me that she was a trained grief counselor. Without asking where she had received her psychology degree, I thanked her for being willing to help.

"I can tell where you are carrying your grief," she pronounced.

"What do you mean?" I asked. "How could you possibly know where I am carrying my grief?"

"If you were carrying your grief close to your heart, you would be big breasted," she replied. I secretly thought, "I wish I had heard this when I was a teenager. It might have made some difference then, but doesn't make any difference now." The counselor then assured me that some of her clients try to throw their grief over their shoulders and end up with a hump in their back. She added, "Some of my clients try to push their grief down and end up without a waistline." By this point, I was sitting up straight and sucking in my stomach.

More importantly, I was trying to remember if I had ever read such concepts in psychology textbooks. You see, I earned a master's degree in counseling and a doctorate degree in educational psychology. I also taught Psychology of the Individual and Psychology of Women at a junior college before coming to Brigham Young University where I taught psychology type classes in the Department of Family Resource

Management in what is now the College of Family, Home and Social Science. In addition, for whatever reason or purpose, I have been gifted with a memory for details and facts stick to me like glue.

As the grief counselor droned on, I started to recall names of textbooks, chapter headings, and class discussions even though my final psychology degree was in 1978 and nearly thirty-three years had come and gone. I reviewed in my mind the works of Freud, Ellis, Skinner, Rogers, and other prominent contributors to the field of psychology, searching specifically for where grief is physically carried. Nowhere could I come up with holding any problem close to the heart, the back, or waistline would make any physical difference. If the grief counselor was correct, she was forging a new trail that prominent psychologists of yesteryear had overlooked. Even Dr. Phil hadn't spoken of this. If she were correct, imagine the revenues that would be lost by plastic surgeons.

I was brought back to the reality of the moment when the grief counselor said, "You need to sit on the floor." Believing her degree in psychology to be more current than mine and that perhaps she was on the cutting edge of new discoveries, in my pencil skirt I made an effort to sit lady-like on the floor. I quietly watched as the counselor placed twenty blank 3x5 cards face-down in front of me. She then said, "Written on the opposite side of each card is one word. Pray about which card you should pick up."

As you can imagine, if I'm complaining about fifty dollars for a non-hair comb by this point I am feeling great irritation with the grief counselor. "I am having trouble getting answers to my prayers," I said. "My husband died. I don't plan to waste a prayer on figuring out which card to pick up."

With coaxing from the counselor, "You can do this," I eventually turned over a 3x5 card that had the word "anger" written on it.

"Why did you choose anger?" the counselor asked.

"Do the other cards read 'murder,' 'rape,' 'abuse,' 'treason'"?

I stood up and prepared to leave. What were the counselor's final words? "I can tell that you are in great sorrow. Your grief is in every cell of your body. I can massage that grief right out of those cells." With that, I walked out the door.

A Licensed Psychologist

Weeks later I was sitting in a sacrament meeting, ignoring the speaker, and thinking about my experience with the counselor. Perhaps I should have called the mortuary to express my disdain at the counseling I had received, but after my experience with the hair issue I decided some other grief-stricken widow could share news about the counselor. I began to ponder—with free time on my hands, meaning no one to care for, no wheelchairs to get in and out of the car, or doctor appointments to keep—perhaps I should grandfather my psychology license from California to Utah and become a practicing psychologist in this state. It was a novel idea, impractical some might say for I was employed as a professor of Church History and Doctrine. I had never practiced as a psychologist after graduating with my master's or doctorate degree. I went straight into teaching. I love the classroom and taught a myriad of subjects from finance to religion to psychology. Why would I teach instead of becoming a clinical psychologist with clients waiting in an outside office? There is an old saying, "Those who can't counsel, teach."

Feeling the old adage applied to me, but knowing that the talent was there as well as the training I went through the hoops of contacting government offices in Sacramento to find out the feasibility of grandfathering my California license to Utah. If you're looking for hoops, phone calls that start with, "Could you hold," and bureaucracy that is uncapped, it is alive and well in the licensing process. However, within a few months I received in the mail a certificate announcing that I was a psychologist licensed to practice in the state of Utah.

Not wanting to be paid for my services, I thought the best place for me to start was as a missionary/volunteer for LDS Social Services. I made an appointment with the director of the LDS Social Services in Provo, Dr. Nathan Gibbons. When I arrived in his office, he put me immediately at ease by telling me the joke of a teenage daughter who had come in for counseling because she hated her mother. Her mother confided in her friend, "I think my daughter likes me better now. The counselor telephoned me today and assured me that my daughter talks about me all the time." I liked the joke and knew I was back in my element—my field of expertise. Without hesitation, I told Dr. Gibbons of my wanting to be a missionary/volunteer at his facility.

Dr. Gibbons paused for the longest time. I think he was stunned by my request. When he finally spoke, Dr. Gibbons said, "Susan, when I think of you, I think of Church History. I think of religion. I think of a professor. As much as I like you, in order to be a missionary volunteer at LDS Social Service, you need a psychology license from the state of Utah."

It was then I handed Dr. Gibbons my license. He held it near the florescent light in his office as if I had handed him a bad two dollar bill or a forged document. I knew he was looking for the official watermark. After concluding the license was genuine, Dr. Gibbons asked the receptionist to call in other psychologists in the clinic and tell them he had a surprise document to show them. Each of the psychologists who entered the office expressed wonder over the certificate and a few held it up to the light. I was a better sport than you might imagine and joined in the merriment. That day Dr. Gibbons invited me to be a missionary psychologist at the LDS Social Services in Provo. I left his office very happy, believing that I could change client's lives for the better.

My first day at the clinic was an eye-opener—a deer in the headlights experience. I had sessions with clients wanting assistance with problems that I had never studied about or been exposed to. For example, no one in the 1970s was addicted to video games. No one was addicted to cellphones. No one had finger-tip access to pornography unless it was a *Playboy* magazine. Few were addicted to Opioids, especially youth growing up in the suburbs with parents who were highly educated.

If you've ever felt unprepared, imagine my horror at realizing that the field of psychology had dramatically moved from what was considered the garden variety of psychological problems—anxiety and depression. There were new problems in the decades since I received my degrees that had propelled more than one psychologist to throw in the towel and seek a different profession.

Back in the director's office, I expressed my inadequacies and my dilemma. I was unprepared for a number of the problems now facing society, but had been set apart by my bishop to be a missionary for LDS Social Services. I spoke with Dr. Gibbons about hating to be a quitter, and hoping there was another way. Talk about a nice man—that was Dr. Nathan Gibbons that day. He invited psychologists and social workers at the clinic to take me under their wing, share their files, DVDs, and techniques. It was as if I were not just re-tooling, but getting a third degree in psychology. Nevertheless, no matter how much assistance and encouragement was given, there remained some clients whose problems I could not address.

My weaknesses were apparent to me. Too many times I reduced myself to the "intake person," meaning I had the first chance to listen to a client and determine the real issue faced by the client, but interrupted the session by saying, "I wish I had the talents to help you, but doctor so-and-so down the hall is the expert in that field. Can I make an appointment for you to see him?"

Less you think I was a total failure as a psychologist, there were two emotional problems that became my specialty. You may have guessed the two already. It is the basic garden-variety problems that bring clients to any counseling center. The first is anxiety and the second is depression. Fortunately, these are the two most treatable emotional problems. This book will focus on a phase of depression—situational depression, the most treatable problem of all.

I am not writing to those who are chronically or clinically depressed—so-called cutters, those who attempt suicide, or have been hospitalized for depression again and again. As the clinically depressed have shared their difficult stories with me, each has a story of depression that has a traceable gradual sliding slope. Their stories are not situational depression. Situational depression begins with a shock response not a gradual sliding slope. It is a momentary setback, a sadness that hurts to the bone.

For example, if you know you will lose a job in six months you have time to think about it. It is not a shock response, it is a gradual response. Call it an office conspiracy to tear you down or merely office politics, or a kiss up kick down administrative style, the result is the same. You will lose your job in six months. For those months, you have the luxury of analyzing your options and evaluating the pros and cons of each option. You can express anger with administrators and assure coworkers you are not receiving your just rewards, but the element of time is on your side. Another example, if the large corporation you work for is transferring you to another location within the year, you and your family have time to absorb the news. Time to surf the internet for housing options, schools for the children, and so forth. If you know the date you will retire, you have time to make plans for your future. Thoughts of such changes may lead to a gradual sliding slop of clinical or chronic depression, but it will not lead to situational depression.

Chronic depression was no doubt the fate of Sisyphus, the king of Ephyra (Corinth), in Greek mythology. Sisyphus surmised that his cleverness surpassed that of the god Zeus. When discovered in his deception, the gods punished Sisyphus for his self-aggrandizing craftiness and condemned him to roll a huge boulder to the top of a hill and watch as the boulder rolled back down the hill. Sisyphus was then to roll the boulder to the top of the hill and again watch as the boulder rolled back down. Sisyphus was condemned to perform these futile actions forever. This is the definition of chronic depression for which there appears no possible redemption. This type of depression is *prolonged* unhappiness. It is debilitating and relentless in its downhill course as much as Sisyphus's boulder. It is as tough an opponent as any trained physician, psychiatrist, or psychologist will ever combat. It is not situational depression.

What is Situational Depression?

We've all experienced situational depression in one way or another—it's the common cold of emotional health. Remember your reaction when you learned that your boyfriend had jilted you for your best friend? You looked at your grades and found your chemistry teacher gave you a "C" when you deserved an "A"? Or you were having a normal day until a policeman came to the door with your honor-student daughter who had been caught stealing alcohol from a local market. Situational depression is always unexpected. It begins by stopping you in your tracks—taking you out of your normal routine.

Illustrating situational depression is best portrayed by an analogy of a stream of murky water composed of disappointments, sorrows, and discouragements lying just below the surface of your everyday life. We can all enjoy happy days and even our best day so far as we surf on top of that water and make it to shore safely at the end of a day even when we know that everything in our lives and the lives of our loved ones is not perfect. As long as the stream, perhaps river or even ocean of disappointment remains below the surface of our lives we can move forward with confidence and happiness. But when situational depression strikes, the shocking event forces the surfer to do a deep dive or in this case an unexpected belly flop into the waters of disappointment, sorrow, and discouragement raging below. Those who stay down in the murky waters risk the likely possibility of embracing chronic depression. Don't chance it!

Situational depression can be just what the name suggests. It is a stop in your everyday routine that inhibits your ability to function normally. It is an emotional jolt that doesn't have to be permanent even though the situation that led to the belly flop may never change. The crisis that hit you suddenly and without warning can be only a shark bite not a devastating drowning if you have the skills to swim to the top. Life's waves will bury any surfer from time to time, but as the book of Ether promises you can come forth again: *"When they were encompassed about by many waters they did cry unto the Lord, and he did bring them forth again"* (Ether 2:17).

Unfortunately, situational depression often strikes when you are at a point in life when everything is going well. You know the adage, "Heartbreaks strike when skies are clear." It's the day when your husband has gone to work, the children are at school, the house is clean, and you decide to sit down and read that mystery novel—then the phone rings with news that undermines your very foundation. How long will situational depression last? Perhaps for you only a few hours, but since you are reading this book perhaps it has lasted longer. For some, the inability to rise above the murky waters lasts a lifetime.

Have you ever wondered why some people glide through life and others hit every bump in the road? Why do some feel only temporarily hopeless and bounce back into life's activities full of energy and creative ideas, ever seeking new avenues for achieving goals while others never rise to the top again?

The answer is—you cannot be a passive participant in rising to the top. The Allied forces in World War II discovered the strength of the Nazi armies by fighting against them, not by surrendering. You will discover the fury of a hurricane by trying to walk against it, not by lying down on the ground. A man who succumbs to the momentary disappointment simply does not know what it would have been like an hour, a week, or a lifetime later if he had faced the disappointment head on. The mythical phoenix crashed and burned, only to rise from its ashes. The example of the resilient phoenix doesn't have to be just a legend for you.

I want to help you navigate when you are thrown off your course—when the very pillars that undergird your happiness, your sense of well-being, are shaken. I want to help you successfully matriculate in society—in life—when your foundation has absorbed a major blow.

Your natural instinct is to withdraw from life and seek shelter in a quiet corner in the house. That's the wrong choice! Depression's breeding ground is agonizing solitude. In that oppressive loneliness, thoughts turn negative and interests in people and events that once held great value to you, diminish. When the joy of life diminishes so does a desire to participate in social events. This is followed by a downward spiral of pessimism that torches the very silver linings of life.

We all know you cannot look at the sun too long. Similarly, you can't stay in the dark abyss of situational depression too long. To do so is to open a trapdoor in your inner self and fall through. It is to wallow in your failures and mistakes, to focus on opportunities squandered, love lost, and time misspent. It is to slog through the mud of unhappiness.

How many hits of unexpected bad news can you take before getting knocked through that trap door? Each of us has a different level of resilience. Some can take a huge number of hits while others get creamed at the first shocking punch. The question is, "Are you ready to fight back?" The answer lies in the next questions. If you are about to get in a cold swimming pool, are you more likely to dive right in or will you inch your way slowly into the pool? If you were to remove a Band-Aid from your arm, do you rip it off or slowly peel it away? If you inch your way into the cold pool, you might conclude the water is too cold and never end up swimming. If you slowly peel the Band-Aid away, the Band-Aid may outlast the sore. Even though you have probably approached getting into a cold pool and removing a Band-Aid both ways, it is now time to dive into the cold water and pull that Band-Aid off quickly, because you are going to battle situational depression as if your life and life's purpose depended on the outcome and perhaps it does.

I now turn to a personal hero of mine—John Huntsman Sr. In 2016 I attended a banquet in Salt Lake City in which athletes were being honored for their significant contributions to sports in the state of Utah. One of the honorees was John Huntsman Sr. Although the master of ceremonies suggested the award given him was because of his athletic prowess in his college days, in his acceptance speech Huntsman assured the assembled guests the award had much more to do with his financial contribution to sports, such as the Huntsman Senior Games. Huntsman accepted the award and sat down after delivering a prepared speech.

As the banquet was coming to a close, the master of ceremonies invited Huntsman to come to the podium and receive a gold ring. This time Huntsman didn't have a prepared speech, but said something that is most significant to each of us as we battle situational depression. "Tomorrow I am going in for my twenty-sixth operation on a recurring problem." Having been seated near him during the ceremonies, I had observed that his blackened hand looked like IV's gone awry. Huntsman then paused and said, "The reason I like sports is because sports taught me that when you fall down, you get up as quick as you can and get back in the game."

The purpose of this book is not to teach you how to fall down. Life has and will continue to teach you that principle again and again. You don't need any help from me. The purpose of this book is to teach you how to get up and get back in the game and continue on your journey of happiness and joy.

CHAPTER TWO

Layers of Emotions

Learning how to get back up when you fall down in the game of life begins by learning that there is a basket of emotions at your fingertips. You would be happier if you had landed on disgust, frustration, or denial when tragedy rocked your world than landing on depression. If you had done so, you would be shelving that unhappy experience in the recesses of your memory as an unpleasant surprise that almost was your undoing, but it was not. It was only a momentary setback.

Unfortunately, situational depression is not just a knee jerk response to bad news. Without being aware of the process, you sifted through layers of negative emotions like shuffling through a deck of playing cards. To understand why depression beat out all other cards in the deck, it is necessary to take a look, albeit brief, at the emotions you experienced before depression set it.

Why depression and not disgust or frustration? The reason you were vulnerable to depression, is because something you care deeply about was lost in the tragedy that shook your world. The loss is more than an item you would have pulled from a burning house. It is what made your world meaningful. It is what defined you. It reflects your value system. Being distraught over the loss and what some call "at your wit's end" is an invitation to open the door to situational depression and to symptoms of full-blown depression.

Symptoms manifest themselves differently much like flu symptoms. When the flu strikes, some people complain of a fever and a headache while others complain of an upset stomach and muscle cramps. Still others report chills, diarrhea, and nausea. Does each person have the flu? Undoubtedly.

Although symptoms of depression may be unique to you, they are not unique to the diagnosis of situational depression. Psychology scholars have developed a universal pattern for diagraming and categorizing the very downward steps a person takes to reach situational depression. Some suggest the universal pattern, tweaked by todays' psychologists, was introduced in 1969 when Elisabeth Kübler-Ross published *On Death and Dying*. In her landmark publication Kübler-Ross concluded all people experience grief and grapple with five emotions—denial, anger, bargaining, depression, and acceptance. She referred to these emotions as stages. "If they only lose their contact lens," Kübler-Ross said, "they still experience the five stages."[1] She argued that to ignore or repress any stage is to become stuck in a stage of unresolved, painful emotion.

Subsequent research has clarified that not everyone stricken with grief experiences all five stages nor will they move through the stages at the same rate, or even in the same order. Although grief is a small slice of a broader range of experiences that may result in situational depression, let us examine this slice to better understand why stage theory with all its warts is still commonplace in psychological therapy today.

Once you begin to look for the stages of denial, anger, bargaining, depression, and acceptance, they pop up everywhere. Are you in the mood for watching old sitcoms?

---

1   Ruth Davis Konigsberg, *The Truth about Grief: The Myth of Its Five Stages and the New Science of Loss* (New York: Simon & Schuster, 2011), 87.

Episodes of *Frasier, The Simpsons, Scrubs, House, The Office,* and *Grey's Anatomy* present characters in various stages of the Kübler-Ross theory. Are you more interested in the news of the day? In 2008 *New York Times* opinion columnist Frank Rich described the US occupation of Iraq as emotional stages: "This war has lasted so long that Americans...have had the time to pass through all five of the Kübler-Ross stages of grief over its implosion."[2] In that same year Lanny Davis, a die-hard Hillary Clinton supporter, lamented Barack Obama's commanding lead in the Democratic primaries: "Denial, yes...Anger, definitely. Bargaining, well, O.K. And depression, that's definitely what I was going through." It wasn't until Obama's acceptance speech at the Democratic closing ceremony that Davis reached "the last stage, acceptance."[3] In 2010, when NBC dumped Conan O'Brien as the *The Tonight Show* host, Conan joked about moving through the stages with a well-trained psychiatrist at his side. The Kübler-Ross theory has become so entrenched in American society that if you want to achieve worthwhile goals, motivational speakers insist steps, usually four or five (but in the case of Stephen Covey seven) as necessary for business success, corporate stability, financial freedom—you name it.

My purpose in presenting the stages is to help you understand the emotions that led to grief and perhaps your situational depression. Although the stages of the Kübler-Ross theory are viewed as antiquated by less seasoned psychologists, their simplicity is helpful in describing the complexity of psychological change. As these stages are presented, keep in mind that your situational depression started with an event or a series of events totally out of your control and unpredictable. It was a rupture, a shocking event that you interpreted as tragic and horrible. It was the event that had an element of fear—threat to life, threat to moral well-being, threat to reputation, or threat of losing property. It was the alarm that shattered the safety

2   Konigsberg, *Truth about Grief,* 2.
3   Konigsberg, *Truth about Grief,* 1.

of your routine. For example, when awakened in an Intensive Care Unit, it matters little whether you turned in the term paper or brought cookies to the party. When the doctor talks of amputating your leg, it makes little difference that you missed last night's curfew or that you made the winning basket in the championship game. When situational depression strikes it is a catastrophic crisis whether your perception of the situation is real or not.

Fight, Flight, or Freeze

Following the shocking event, a period of numbness sets in that lasts for twenty-four to thirty-six hours. (Numbness in this case is best defined as "devoid of sensation" and "devoid of emotion.") Some find the answer for numbness is to lay down in bed with the hope that sleep will lessen the pain. Some slump in a chair and gaze out a window at an unseen object. Still others turn to social media, hoping a familiar voice will help them deal with their fears or turn to blogs, podcasts, and Internet radio shows to rally masses to their side. Others fantasize about how things should have been and become almost paralytic with the loss of hope.

When life goes awry, sadness follows numbness and gains a footing before coping mechanisms finely tuned through childhood, youth, and adulthood kick in. The first mechanism to respond is fight, flight, or freeze. In the animal kingdom survival depends on being able to outfight, outrun, and outsmart all predators. Panicked herds of antelope run from lions and monkeys screech at snakes slithering up trees. Much like the startled animals that either move with great agility or remain in place watching the predator's next move, all of us experience in one way or another fight, flight, and freeze.

Fight is a combative stance—a desire to strike back. Flight is the desire to run away from an uncomfortable situation. As a general rule, men fight and women flee. Said differently, "Men go to war and women go shopping." Situational depression has much more to do with freeze in place than either fight or flight.

As raging storms have pelted your world, you've had more than one occasion to fight back or take flight. You've probably stepped on emotionally laden electric wires without getting knocked to the ground. Perhaps you've maneuvered through a disturbing maze of heartaches—death in the family, loss of a job, untimely illness, a wayward daughter, and divorce without succumbing to situational depression. Why is it different now? You're older. Coping mechanisms learned in childhood don't necessarily work for a lifetime. You can take only so many steps on that electric wire before being knocked to the ground.

According to the *Diagnostic and Statistical Manual of Mental Disorders* (DSM) published by the American Psychiatric Association, "Your sadness doesn't become depression until it has settled in for a while . . . two weeks."[4] In that two week interim loved ones and associates offer sympathy. Most are willing to listen as the widow mourns the loss of her departed husband. However, when the widow is still mourning a year or twenty years later, the patience of even her closest relatives grows thin. In our modern society, sorrows are to be experienced not to be retold at the least provocation. The widow is expected to move on—find new interests, joy, and happiness. When a widow bursts into tears at an unexpected moment, a friend may ask, "Can I help?" Through her sobs the widow speaks of her loss decades before. The friend may turn to her in disgust and say, "Move on! He's gone! Get over it! You're living in the past!"

Centuries ago widows were expected to wear dresses of black bombazine and mourning bonnets with black crepe veils. Bracelets woven from strands of the deceased hair, black armbands, and black-border stationery were expected. These outward signs of mourning are vestiges of the past but not acceptable today. Although the widow may never

---

4   Gary Greenberg, *Manufacturing Depression: The Secret History of a Modern Disease* (New York: Simon & Schuster, 2010), 34.

end her mourning, she is expected to move on and become a contributing, vital member of society. She, like all of us, is expected to push through the Kübler-Ross stages of grief and emerge triumphant, ready to face head-on life with all its bumps.

The Stages

You, like the grieving widow to some extent, pass through the Kübler-Ross stages of denial, anger, bargaining, depression, and acceptance not just once, but many times. In your case, as you were moving through the stages for the umpteenth time, you were snagged by depression—not the full blown depression with all its invasive downsides but situational depression. As you read about the stages, consider why you set up camp, built a bonfire, and decided to stay for a night or two if not more in the beginning stage of depression.

Denial

The first word people say when confronted with bad news is "No!" followed by "I don't believe it!" and "It can't be true!" Next comes the anecdotal reason for such assurance: "My husband is not in a hotel in Chicago with his secretary, he is visiting his mother in Atlanta." "My son has gone to the movies with Brian, he is not with his girlfriend at the lake." "My dog never leaves the yard and would not have bitten your child." "My best friend would never tell such a secret to anyone."

Denial is nature's way of letting into your psyche only as much bad news as you can process. To deny the reality of bad news beyond the initial shock, is to put grief and reality on hold. Delaying grief does have its benefits—the most important being to preserve the pillars of your world. But denial can buy only temporary relief. A certificate of death, a bill of divorcement, a letter from the principal confirming the truancy, or an arrest warrant forces reality to take center stage.

Those who remain in denial, refusing to face the disappointments of reality, live a Pollyanna life—floating through life cheerful not knowing that much of life is passing them by. Take for instance this Pollyanna scenario: "Your daughter wrecked the family car and parked it in the garage. She went to bed, confident that when she wakes up the car is not damaged and is safely parked in the garage. She just had a bad dream." Try this scene: "The gossip going around school today was that John asked my best friend to the high school prom," Margaret says to her mother. "I'm going to my room to get a jumpstart on my homework. I'll leave my phone with you. Call me when John texts. We'll both get a big laugh about the rumor." Or this story of the young boy who wanted to be a baseball player:

> With the desire to become the next mighty ballplayer, [a very young boy] decided to go outside and practice. He held the baseball in one hand and the bat in the other, and he threw the ball into the air. With a wish to hit the ball as far as he could, he took a great swing, but the ball fell to the ground without even touching the wood of the bat. Not to be denied, he went at it again. As he was about to throw the ball in the air, his determination grew as the thought of a powerful hit came into his mind. But alas, the results were the same. The ball lay on the ground. But as any good ballplayer knows, you have three strikes before you are out. He concentrated even more, threw the ball in the air, and gave the mightiest swing he had ever attempted. As the ball again fell to the ground, the tears began to swell in his eyes. Then all of a sudden a great smile appeared, and he said, "What a pitcher!"[5]

You'll like this scenario best—the woman who defies the aging process. You've seen the look—facelifts, breast-implants,

---

5   James B. Martino, "All Things Work Together for Good," *Ensign*, May 2010.

laser surgery, Botox, blond hair, and lots of jewelry. She may deny, even to herself, that she is aging but she hasn't fooled anyone except St. Peter.

"How much time do I have on earth," the aging woman asked St. Peter. "You've got fifteen years, two months and three days." The woman thanked St. Peter and checked herself into a hospital and demanded a complete makeover. A few weeks later, a dazzling beauty walked out of the hospital and was hit by a bus and dies. When she meets St. Peter at the pearly gates, the woman confronts him: "You told me I had fifteen years, two months and three days to live!" St. Peter replies, "I'm sorry! I didn't recognize you."

Life isn't meant to be like Dorothy in The Wizard of Oz clicking her feet and red slippers magically appearing. Life isn't a secret garden or anything else hidden behind a closet or in the next room. Reality, with all of its imperfections, is where sanity makes its greatest stand against denial. Yet for each of you, a momentary passage through denial with all of its "No's" leads to the next stage. It seems odd to say in print, but "Congratulations, you successfully passed through denial and are on to the Kübler-Ross stage of anger.

Anger

The angry person asks, "Why me?" There are answers for who, what, when, where, and how but often only God knows "why."

"Why am I being picked on when I am the best employee my boss ever hired? I am never late for work. My accounting strategy saved the company thousands of dollars. The boss always has something nice to say to me."

"Why am I overlooked for administrative positions? I'm a natural leader—always have been and always will be. Ask anyone. I make decisions quickly and get the job done.

Intuitively, I have the correct solution to problems before the discussion ends."

"Why is my child running with the wrong crowd? I've been a terrific father. I sat in the bleachers on snowy days and cheered him on when other fathers didn't even show up for the game. I even cancelled an important business trip to drive him and his friends to scout camp."

"Why was I diagnosed with lung cancer? I have never smoked a cigarette in my life?"

"I have worked hard, been honest in my financial dealings, and still can't afford a new car. My friend brags about finding a loophole in the tax code and cheats the government. He has a new car and a big house. He isn't even a good employee."

"My daughter studies every night, turns her homework in on time, and still can't get above a "D" in algebra. Helen's daughter never brings home schoolwork. She spends too much time texting friends, and has an "A" in algebra.

The answer to these and hundreds of similar questions is, "I don't know." Ask any angry person, they don't know either. Life is unfair. The old adage, "The rain falls on the just and unjust" is never far from any lip. "Is there justice in this life?" In the heat of the moment, the answer is an emphatic, "No!"

Anger results from being profoundly blocked. If you have trouble recalling a time when you were profoundly blocked, phone your cable provider. An automated voice will answer and ask a series of questions. Although you repeat the word "Operator," the automated voice replies, "I don't understand." After answering questions about your name, phone number, security code, network carrier, and so forth, you hear the automated words "I'll transfer you now." You breathe a sigh of relief knowing you will get help. Then the automated voice starts over with a series of questions that begin with, "Are you still there?" When you are connected to that "live person" residing in Malaysia, you are asked the same questions before being told about a red button on the transmitter and some numbers on the television monitor. It is then the call is disconnected. This is the definition of being "profoundly blocked." On the freeway it is called "road rage" and at home "unacceptable behavior."

Anger does not solve an impasse, but it does reveal pain—your pain. When my grandson wants ice cream before dinner or his sister to stop playing with his toys or stop staring at him, he screams, yells, and throws a fit. His father says, "Use your words"—meaning don't yell, scream, or throw a fit to show your pain. Talk about it. The advice is easy to give but difficult to follow when you are young and when you are old. No one likes being told what to do. Advice is cheap so they say, but there is no stopping the ill-informed advisor.

There is another issue. Asking someone you love to move through anger to a happier place is alienating—just ask Heather. Her brother, concerned over her outward display of anger following the suicidal death of her daughter, said, "Be careful that your anger does not evoke the wrath of God." Heather yelled, "What is He going to do? Take my daughter away? What's he going to do, take me?" The brother knelt down by her side and said, "I'm going to pray for you so that you will soften your angry feelings." At that moment Heather told her brother to get out of her house and made the decision that church was no longer for her. It took years before Heather returned to worship service and even more years before she attended a family gathering.[6]

Pouting and insisting that you have the right to be angry is childish, but you do have the right to acknowledge that life is unfair. To deal with the unfairness, look for a socially acceptable outlet. Pounding bread dough, playing Beethoven's Fifth, and walking miles up and down the street won't solve your anger or blocked goals, but it helps. Positive outlets for anger have produced cleaner houses, cleaner garages, gardens weeded, floors vacuumed, and so forth. Putting it in another

---

6   Elisabeth Kubler-Ross and David Kessler, *On Grief and Grieving: Finding the Meaning of Grief through the Five Stages of Loss* (New York: Scribner, 2005), 14.

way, your husband needs his woodshop and you need that sewing machine. But at some point, if anger is still winning even those outlets will fail.

Anger needs to be dealt with before it leads to bigger problems, for anger chips away at the strength of even the best families. President Thomas S. Monson told the story of a couple who were having a disagreement while driving to a relative's house. The disagreement "became so heated that they were yelling at one another." Their toddler in the backseat of the car started to cry. His crying fueled the husband's anger. "Losing total control of his temper, he picked up a toy the child had dropped on the seat and flung it in the direction of his wife. He missed hitting his wife. Instead, the toy struck their son, with the result that he was brain damaged." President Monson concluded the story by saying, "Anger doesn't solve anything. It builds nothing, but it can destroy everything."[7]

What am I trying to say—don't hold onto anger. Although you have a good reason for being angry, let it go—if not permanent at least put it on the back burner. Apparently, on some level you did just that for you are not stuck in anger. You successfully stepped through denial and anger and moved onto step three—bargaining.

Bargaining

In the movie *Napoleon Dynamite*, Uncle Rico laments the outcome of a high school football game. He fantasizes that his life would have been better if he had thrown the winning touchdown pass. Believing that going back in time to that all-crucial game would fix his life's problems, Rico submitted himself to his nephew's time machine. Perhaps you, like Uncle Rico, would like to change something if not everything in your life. You've had the occasion to say, "If only" or "What if?"

---

7   Thomas S. Monson, "School Thy Feelings, O My Brother," *Ensign*, November 2009.

"If only I could lose weight."

"If only I had stopped at the stop sign."

"If only I had passed the LSAT exam."

"What if I were more beautiful?"

"What if I had been a better father, son, or husband?"

"What if I had not told that lie?"

Frequent usage of the phrase "if only" or "what if" leads to an expected outcome by inserting the word "then."

"If I had been a better lover then my husband would not be looking over the fence."

"If had paid my parking tickets then I wouldn't be searching on google for an attorney to defend me."

"If only I had accepted Tim's marriage proposal then I would be living in a mansion instead of waiting on tables."

"If only I hadn't yelled at my daughter then I would know where she is tonight."

In each example "then" is the consequence of the "if only" or "what if" fantasy.

Much like Uncle Rico or Peter Pan and his lost boys, you can get stuck wishing a portion, if not all of your life were different. Leaders of corporations and nations stumble not because they have an occasional unfulfilled wish but "because they get *hooked* by them, like a fish caught on a line."[8] To put it bluntly, if you live your life rehearsing lost dreams sooner or later you will find yourself at a bargaining table in need of a mediator.

For those with religious leanings the table is the throne of God. For those with less than a religious bent, the old saying "There are no atheists in the foxhole" still applies.[9] When under enemy fire and facing the threat of imminent death, no one fantasizes of what might have been. "Please, God" is the urgent plea.

---

8   Christine Carter, *The Sweet Spot: How to Find Your Grove at Home and Work* (New York: Ballantine Books, 2015), 216.

9   Bryan Walsh, "Does Spirituality Make Us Happy?" *Time* (New York: Time Inc., 2017), 84.

Such heartfelt cries for help are often the subject of stories shared at General Conference—the lost boy, the car accident, and the discouraging diagnosis. In October 2012 Elder David S. Baxter shared the story of a divorced single mother of seven children ranging in ages from seven to sixteen. The mother had gone across the street to deliver something to a neighbor and looked back at her home. Elder Baxter quoted the mother as saying,

> As I turned around to walk back home, I could see my house lighted up. I could hear echoes of my children as I had walked out of the door a few minutes earlier. They were saying: 'Mom, what are we going to have for dinner?' 'Can you take me to the library?' 'I have to get some poster paper tonight.' Tired and weary, I looked at that house and saw the light on in each of the rooms. I thought of all of those children who were home waiting for me to come and meet their needs. My burdens felt heavier than I could bear.

> "I remember looking through tears toward the sky, and I said, 'Dear Father, I just can't do it tonight. I'm too tired. I can't face it. I can't go home and take care of all those children alone. Could I just come to You and stay with You for just one night?'[10]

Although each story presented at conference is different, the outcome is the same. The Lord steps in and answers the urgent plea in a miraculous manner.

Although this is what you may want—a miracle—at this point it does not appear forthcoming. Aesop of *Aesop's Fables* describes this as good news: "We would often be sorry if our

---

10 David S. Baxter, "Faith, Fortitude, Fulfillment: A Message to Single Parents," *Ensign*, May 2012.

wishes were gratified."[11] Because you heartily disagree, the bargaining process begins.

The typical approach to bargaining is not dissimilar to "If … then"—the approach used to fantasize how your past might have been different. You may bargain with the Lord by promising to give more money, faithfully keep His commandments, and be on time to all Church meetings. Perhaps the following is your approach:

"Not satisfied with ten percent tithing? If I gave eleven or twelve percent will you solve the problem?"

"I haven't written in my journal since I was a missionary, but if I wrote in my journal every day for a month could I have your attention?"

"I haven't read the scriptures daily, attended the temple weekly, done my ministering assignment, you know the list, but if I did would you intervene in my behalf?"

When nothing miraculous, meaning out of the realm of normalcy, occurs situational depression follows or what Kübler-Ross calls the beginning of step four.

Depression

Depression is anger turned inward or as Spanish philosopher George Santayana said, "Depression is rage spread thin."[12] Depression is a selfish illness that withdraws the extended hand, for there is no time to think of others. Trapped in a timeless, unending nightmare with nothing that breaks the deadening spell of depression leaves the sufferer weary, stale, and flat. Like an animal, who senses the cold gloom of day and moves into a dark cave, the depressed find caves of their own. Call it a bedroom, a television room, or a video room, it

---

11   David S. Awbrey, *Finding Hope in the Age of Melancholy* (Boston: Little, Brown and Company, 1999), 36.
12   Blaise A. Aquirre, *Depression: Biographies of Disease* (Westport, Connecticut: Greenwood Press, 2008), 5.

is one in the same—a place to escape, to sleep, watch hours of mindless television, or reach one more level in a senseless maze of video games.

When the depressed moves away from the cave, symptoms of depression betray his despair—walks slow as if carrying a great burden on his shoulders, speaks in labored tones and is slow in speech as if searching for words, mental processes are sluggish, and intellectual acuity impaired. Simple problems, like adding a column of numbers, are a tedious and painful chore. Routine activities such as brushing teeth, cutting fingernails, eating, bathing, and dressing are a burden.

"Do you want to get something to eat?" The depressed person slowly answers, "No."

"Do you want to get out of bed?" "No."

"Shall I invite friends over for a pizza party?" "No."

"Can I open the drapes so you can see the beautiful day?" "No."

"Do you want to see a movie? A new *Star Wars* movie is playing at the theater?" "No."

If a chance conversation does ensue, the depressed will speak pessimistically about family and friends interjecting bitter, sarcastic, and cutting remarks. Being bitter, sarcastic, and ornery doesn't border on being unkind, it is unkind. Friends will take flight. Family members, too. Appointments and activities will be reduced. Incoming texts and phone calls will drop to a need to know basis.

Although the depressed wants nothing more than to be left alone that is not the right scenario. When alone, like a worthless penny in a coin sorter, the penny will drop into a designated slot and be pronounced worthless. The medical diagnosis for feelings of worthlessness is depression. The diagnosis gives the depressed license to brood over failures, be self-critical, and to own feelings of worthlessness.

If this is a description of you, change for depression has come to stay with a room all its own and maid service at her beck and call. You don't want to become the teenager who hugs the walls at school, sits alone at lunch, and retreats to video games at home nor do you want to be the elderly man who counts holes in the ceiling tiles at the rest home.

For F. Scott Fitzgerald the worst possible time for depression was night: "In a real dark night of the soul it is always three o'clock in the morning."[13] For those with situational depression, the worst time is the daylight hours when, like the Peanuts' character Pig-Pen, a dark cloud hovers overhead. The cloud never becomes darkest just before it is totally black, it merely becomes a permanent extension of Pig-Pen. Situational depression is the dark cloud. In your case, it is not something seen as much as the absence of something not seen—light.

"Who gets depressed?—good people, nice people, proper people. Those who do not care one way or the other do not suffer from depression. That may be the first positive thing I've said in the depression stage. Let me repeat it—you have to be a good, caring person to become depressed. The problem is once you have experienced a bout of depression, it is easy to return to it and get stuck. For those who are stuck, therapy becomes the norm. As for anti-depressant pills, can't leave home without them.

It is difficult to live with a person stuck in the angry stage due to the real possibility of verbal and physical abuse. It is difficult to live with the Pollyanna type who smiles through life while denying reality. But the most difficult person to live with is the acutely depressed. Ultimately, the depressed will conclude that he is just taking up space—he has no purpose, no meaning, and no hope. That is the extreme of depression—it is not you.

Acceptance

Eventually the depressed person will emerge from his cave— the bathroom and the kitchen can't be ignored. He will return

---

13   Michel Mok, "The Other Side of Paradise: F. Scott Fitzgerald, 40, Engulfed in Despair," *New York Post*, September 25, 1936.

to a normal routine like work, school, and activities. Could it be said, "He has accepted his loss and moved on to find happiness?" Acceptance is not forgetting a loss or implying that you have glossed over a hurt. Acceptance is not saying, "I'm okay with what happened." Acceptance is not shrugging your shoulders and asking, "What else can I do? I have to accept what happened and move on." Acceptance is knowing that you will not get over your loss but you will learn to live with it. By so doing you establish a new norm—a new definition of self.

Too many in the acceptance stage give the outward pretense of a happy, prosperous life but inwardly struggle. In many respects they mirror a "Potemkin Village."

> In the late 18th century, Catherine the Great of Russia announced she would tour the southern part of her empire, accompanied by several foreign ambassadors. The governor of the area, Grigory Potemkin, desperately wanted to impress these visitors. And so he went to remarkable lengths to showcase the country's accomplishments.
>
> For part of the journey, Catherine floated down the Dnieper River, proudly pointing out to the ambassadors the thriving hamlets along the shore, filled with industrious and happy townspeople. There was only one problem: it was all for show. It is said that Potemkin had assembled pasteboard facades of shops and homes. He had even positioned busy-looking peasants to create the impression of a prosperous economy. Once the party disappeared around the bend of the river, Potemkin's men packed up the fake village and rushed it downstream in preparation for Catherine's next pass."[14]

---

14   Dieter F. Uchtdorf, "On Being Genuine," *Ensign*, May 2015.

To be satisfied with the life of a "Potemkin Village" is to live an unfortunate, counterfeit life, for one day you will again face the Kübler-Ross stages of loss—denial, anger, bargaining, depression, and acceptance. This time you will know that the stage of acceptance is false, for you can still go from feeling on top of the world one minute to devastation the next. This is because your acceptance of what happened was disingenuous.

It takes time to reach real acceptance, especially when gaping wounds are slow to heal. Time may dull wounds, but wounds are still there. More than one man still mournfully sings, "Nobody knows the troubles I've seen. Nobody knows my sorrows."

My hope is that you are ready to begin the process of moving away from stage theory. Not everyone is capable of such a move for it requires taking down coping mechanisms that worked in the past but are no longer working. Robert Frost cautioned against such a move: "Don't ever take a fence down until you know why it was put up."[15] In grief groups, the rule about tearing down fences is connected to the rule about tissues: "Everyone has to grab their own tissues." When a group member cries, no one in the group is permitted to jump up and reach for the tissue box. After all, such an action says, "Hurry and stop crying."[16]

I will not be reaching for the tissues or saying to you, "Hurry up and stop crying. The world is moving forward and you need to catch up." I won't help you tear down a fence until a sturdy fence has been constructed. I won't say, "I told you so" when symptoms of situational depression begin to disappear. What I will do is help you break the chains of depression and find happiness that has eluded you too long.

---

15   Steven Jay Lynn, et.al., *Health, Happiness, and Well Being: Better Living through Psychological Science* (Los Angeles: Sage, 2015), 299.
16   Ross and Kessler, *On Grief and Grieving*, 46.

CHAPTER THREE

You're Not Alone

When it comes to situational depression, you are not alone. Situational depression has been around since the beginning of time. Ever wondered how Adam and Eve felt after partaking of the forbidden fruit and being thrust out of the Garden of Eden? What about other biblical characters like Saul and King David? Oh, and don't forget Eleanor Roosevelt, Winston Churchill, or Abraham Lincoln. On January 23, 1841, Lincoln wrote to his law partner, John T. Stuart, "I am the most miserable man living. If what I feel were equally distributed to the whole human family, there would not be one cheerful face on the earth. Whether I shall ever be better I cannot tell....To remain as I am is impossible; I must die or be better, it appears to me."[17]

Ask anyone if they've had a bout of situational depression; they will tell you of an emotionally devastating experience that was nearly their undoing, but they will tell you that they survived. Although this type of depression takes its toll on felons, rock stars, CIA agents, and basketball coaches, it is

---

17   "Letter to John Stuart, January 23, 1841," in Ray Baster, ed., *Collected Works of Abraham Lincoln*, 9 vols. (New Brunswick, New Jersey: Rutgers University Press, 1953), 1:230.

not their undoing. There is always another jail term to serve, another concert to present, another foreign spy to catch, and yet another game to win. For them, as for all of us, situational depression was just a momentary stumbling block along the journey of life.

Although situational depression is a well-known malady today, it took centuries for the situational aspect of depression to be clearly defined. For example, in the 1940s, the most accepted explanation for this type of depression was, "She doesn't feel well tonight." When pressed for why she did not feel well, the proverbial answer was, "She's tired. She needs her rest." How could a husband in the 1940s admit that his wife was depressed when the expectation was a chicken in every pot and a car in every garage—not to mention health, prosperity, and happiness?[18] To suggest a wife is depressed when her husband is handsome, a good provider, and great at flipping burgers on a barbeque would not only put a cloud over his wife, but would also vilify him as a husband.

Situational depression for most members of American society, especially the affluent, was the best-kept family secret. When pressed about why your wife misses every family function, the best advice was, "Don't hang your dirty laundry out for the neighbors to see" or "Put your poker face on." The appearance of the abundant life was valued, and "keeping up with the Joneses, the Rockefellers, or the next-door neighbor" was all important. Any untoward action that might send your wife headlong into a massive fight-or-flight response was to be avoided at all costs. Appearances were everything.

Behind closed doors and the hype of happiness blasted on radio and shouted from newsstands, physicians quietly treated those who suffered from situational depression. Unfortunately, they did so without rapid results or much success. Bloodletting, opiates, sleep therapy, electric shock, straightjackets, hot

---

18   See Binford Winston Gilbert, *The Pastoral Care of Depression: A Guidebook* (New York: Haworth Pastoral Press, 1998), 75.

baths, cold baths, and special diets of protein or lack thereof were offered as the beat-all answer without the stamp of approval from society or the scientific community. By the time the physician had tried his umpteenth remedy, situational depression had moved to prolonged sadness, with more than one patient dead and others permanently scarred.

Fearful that their remedies might result in lawsuits, physicians turned to advice under the guise of the fancy title "physiological counseling."[19] When the patients' symptoms grew worse, physicians raised prices, harped on the faults of the patient in not "working" enough to get better, or passed the depressed on to a resented colleague just for spite. Remember the movie *What about Bob*? Then, of course, there was always the exit plan where the physician could say good-bye to the patient. That plan included an asylum whose caregivers sported white coats and labeled prolonged sadness as "crazy."

A few proverbial researchers tried to do more than pronounce the sad "crazy." They described with seeming clarity situational depression as the elephant in the room when they had uncovered only the trunk. Their prescriptions were hailed as the norm, something that uncannily slowed and then halted further empirical studies.[20] With too many false dogmatic statements prevailing, understanding how situational depression evolved into prolonged sadness progressed in fits and spurts. At its best, patients improved as did standard care. At its worst, treatment guidelines harmed rather than cured. Too often patients left medical facilities concerned that all discretionary funds were spent and they were not any better.

It was not until 1972 that a focus on situational depression became the "hotbed topic" of public interest. As the old saying goes, in that year "the cat was let out of the bag." Being

---

19   Nathan S. Kline, *From Sad to Glad: Kline on Depression* (New York: G. P. Putnam's Sons, 1974), 28.

20   Allan M. Leventhal and Christopher R. Martell, *The Myth of Depression as Disease: Limitations and Alternatives to Drug Treatment* (Westport, Connecticut: Praeger, 2006), ix.

momentary or profoundly sad would never again remain the family secret—like Bo Radley, the star in *To Kill a Mockingbird*, hiding in a basement or up in an attic was no longer acceptable. It was time to come out of the dark recesses of home into the light of the day. As one by one faces of the depressed were seen on streets in Salt Lake City, Chicago, and Los Angeles, one acclaimed columnist couldn't refrain from writing, "Never have so many people been unhappy. A public poll has shown that one out of two people is depressed much or some of the time."[21] Another suggested there were millions of Americans "sliding into the black hole of depression, powerless to stop their descent."[22] A nation asked if such could be true.

Citizens were shocked when public figures like author William Styron, newscaster Mike Wallace, and humorist Art Buchwald tossed aside societal norms and made their depression public. They hoped to get the message across that "depression is a recognized, treatable medical illness, just like pneumonia or a broken leg."[23]

Today, depression is so rampant that not just millions but tens of millions of Americans suffer from one form of depression or another. The bottom line—you're not alone. But there is little comfort in that fact. It is not like you just won the lottery. You have joined an ever-growing group of Americans— now estimated at 50 million—who live in an opulent society and on the surface should be on their knees thanking God for the abundance in their lives. Instead, tears are commonplace, hearts are broken, and pleas for happiness ascend daily to heaven. The medical cost for such lamenting, hours missed at work, and loss of life is about $40 billion annually.[24] Depression—even

---

21 Gilbert, *Pastoral Care of Depression*, 1.
22 Richard Dayringer, et al., *Dealing with Depression: Five Pastoral Interventions* (New York: The Haworth Pastoral Press, 1995), 1.
23 Malcolm Noell McLeod, *Lifting Depression: The Chromium Connection* (Laguna Beach, California: Basic Health Publications, Inc., 2005), 20.
24 Gabriel Cousens and Mark Mayell, *Depression-Free for Life: A Physician's All-Natural, 5-Step Plan* (New York City: Harper and Collins, 2001), 5.

situational depression—is a big business. Do pharmaceutical companies benefit? Doctors? Hospitals? You bet. Do you? NO! It is an ill-afforded expenditure, an out-of-pocket expense that can wreck any budget.

What has caused such an upsurge in depression nationwide? Death of a loved one is one cause, for no life insurance check can take the place of someone who has shared "your most intimate hopes, fears, and dreams."[25] Divorce, with all its ugly ramifications, ranks high as a cause of depression, as do childhood problems (such as sexual abuse) that leave gaping emotional wounds.[26] A genetic component like a family history of depression predisposes the likelihood of another family member contracting the malady. For example, when an identical twin becomes depressed, there is a high probability that the other twin will also become depressed.[27] Age is another factor. Living alone, lack of social support, and a lower socioeconomic status are also contributing factors.[28] And so the studies go.

Who is most likely to suffer from situational depression? Women are two to three times more likely than men to have a bout. Why are women more depressed than men? Because women are more likely to seek medical help than men. Women will reveal to their doctor depressive symptoms and receive a diagnosis. Men, on the other hand, may have the same tendency toward depression but see symptoms as a sign of weakness, so they refuse to tell any medical physician. Instead of seeking help, they become irritable, angry, and drink heavily.[29]

---

25 Robert L. Veninga, *A Gift of Hope: How We Survive Our Tragedies* (New York: Ballantine Books, 1987), 46.

26 McLeod, *Lifting Depression*, 16.

27 McLeod, *Lifting Depression*, 17.

28 James M. Ellison, Helen H. Kyomen, and David G. Harper, "Depression in Later Life: An Overview with Treatment Recommendations," in David L. Mintz, ed., *Psychiatric Clinics of North America 35*, no. 1 (March 2012): 204.

29 Aguirre, *Depression: Biographies of Disease*, 46.

Situational depression is so universal today that portraying it in the extreme on the silver screen has made more than one producer, director, and film star a billionaire. *A Beautiful Mind* won an Oscar for Best Movie in 1991, and *The English Patient* in 1996 also won an Oscar. *As Good as it Gets* (1997) and *One Flew Over the Cuckoos Nest* (1975) were box office hits. Nicole Kidman's role as the depressed Virginia Woolf in *The Hours* (2003) was hands-down terrific. Although portraying mental illness delights audiences worldwide, it never delights the sufferer.

Of the various types of mental illness, you're in luck—situational depression is the most treatable. It is the common cold of mental illness. In other words, wait two weeks and it will go away—or get a prescription for ten days of high-dose vitamin C or an over-the-counter nasal spray and solve the problem.

Unfortunately, it is not always that simple, especially when it is kept on the front burner of life. One client described situational depression after two weeks like "walking in molasses." Another claimed, "I am stuck in a long, gray winter with no spring." Famed psychologist Alex Korb's description of situational depression resonates with me: "Being tuned to the six o'clock news *all the time*. If that was all you watched, you'd start to think the whole world was full of nothing but political scandals, weather disasters, and horrific crimes. If you could only change the channel, you'd see everything else that's out there—but you can't."[30]

What these descriptions convey is that when situational depression rears its ugly head, its victim is stuck and can't move forward. Imagine millions of American citizens stuck and immobile. Why? Their thoughts have stuffed them into a time warp with no escape hatch. In such a paralyzing state, it becomes a burden to want to live for another tomorrow that is only more

---

30   Alex Korb, *The Upward Spiral: Using Neuroscience to Reverse the Course of Depression, One Small Change at a Time* (Oakland, California: New Harbinger Publications, Inc., 2015), 54.

of the same. Writer F. Scott Fitzgerald wrote on his darkest day, "Every act of life, from the morning toothbrush to the friend at dinner, became an effort. I hated the night when I couldn't sleep and I hated the day because it went toward night."[31] For Truman Capote, feelings of sameness or hopelessness led him to say, "When you've got nowhere to turn, turn on the gas."[32] Let me make it clear—suicide is never the answer. Suicide is a permanent solution to a temporary problem.

There is always an answer for a temporary problem. I can punch holes in my client's claim that "No matter how I slice depression, the biggest problem with the downward spiral is that it doesn't just get me down, it keeps me down."[33] Even the aging client wreaks with falsehood when lamenting that depression has eroded her love until even the memory of love fades like faces in old photographs and no longer seems familiar.[34]

For the boxer who suffers one blow after another and lays down on the mat rather than stand up to suffer yet another blow, the solution is to get out of the ring.[35] For the dancer who breaks her leg and is told she will never dance again, the solution is new vistas. For the businessman who takes out bankruptcy, there is always a better business model to follow. There is more than one note to play on a keyboard and more than one club in a golf bag—opportunity awaits but, as the saying goes, "Time waits for no man."

The time for you is now. There is a new world to explore filled with challenges and surprises. There is a new battle to win, and this one can be won. It is time to move on and stop the disappointments and sorrows of yesterday from taking your present and future. Are you willing to abandon your bed of nails? It won't be easy, but it will be worth it. Your next step is to make and keep an appointment with a family physician.

---

31   Aguirre, Depression: *Biographies of Disease*, 34.
32   Truman Capote quote in Aguirre, *Depression: Biographies of Disease*, 3.
33   Korb, *The Upward Spiral*, 3.
34   Aguirre, *Depression: Biographies of Disease*, 132.
35   Veninga, *Gift of Hope*, 60.

CHAPTER FOUR

The Family Doctor

You wouldn't think of waiting for a family member with high cholesterol and high blood pressure to have a stroke before you suggested or even insisted he seek medical help. Is there a reason you hesitate to make an appointment to see a doctor? Is it the childhood memory of kicking and screaming over a tetanus shot or an x-ray? I know the waiting room will be crowded with patients who cough, have communicable diseases, and are holding screaming babies, but make the appointment anyway. If you have good insurance, seeing the doctor will be cheaper than a swing through Walmart.

Why do I insist that the family doctor is the next step? Untreated depressive illness can lead to personal, family, and social disasters. You don't want that! In addition, without treatment, painful symptoms can last for weeks, months, or years. One suffering youth said, "People only see the spiked hair and chains; they don't see 'me.' If they could, they'd realize that the only difference between us is that I wear my pain on the outside."[36]

36   Gilbert, *Pastoral Care of Depression*, 85.

Knowing when to see a doctor is all important—

Two parents took a little boy to his first symphony concert. He became fascinated with the musician who played the cymbals and thought it would be great fun to be able to grow up and clang the cymbals like he did. After the performance the parents took the little boy backstage where he talked with his favorite hero, the cymbal player. He asked the musician, "What do you have to know in order to play the cymbals?" This was a tough question. The musician thoughtfully considered the sincere query from the little boy. After a few moments he slowly said, "The one thing you must know is when."[37]

If your sadness hasn't diminished in two weeks, it is "when." Confucius said, "The journey of a thousand miles begins with a single step."[38] That single step is to call your doctor.

It can be a difficult step, for as "a general rule, people find it much easier to talk about a physical complaint than an emotional one," even with a trained physician.[39] For example, if you broke your leg before a ski race, the doctor and even avid fans would understand why you opted out of the race. If given the chance, you would share details of how you broke your leg and your frustration at missing the race. But when you're feeling down, the tendency is to hold back. This is not the time to hold back or be secretive.

To make and keep a doctor's appointment is to make the decision that isolation is not an option. You are willing to seek outside help. This decision trumps saying, "Leave me alone! You don't understand what I am going through." It beats accepting depression with what some call a "stiff upper lip."

Doctors know that there are a number of "factors, ranging from genetics to the side effects of prescription drugs" that

---

37   Gilbert, *Pastoral Care of Depression*, 57.
38   Korb, *Upward Spiral*, 96.
39   Aguirre, *Depression: Biographies of Disease*, 129.

cause depression. They also know that medical disorders are notorious for masquerading as depression; these include, but are not limited to, deficiencies in Vitamin D, hormonal imbalance, and thyroid problems.[40] In order for the doctor to rule out your situational depression as being medically caused, it is important to have a complete medical exam.[41]

As much as I know the doctor is the clinch pin and the medical exam is all-important, I want you to be wary. Too often, doctors "tout certainty at the expense of truth, especially when what they are certain about is something so complex, baffling and weighty" as depression.[42] It was George Bernard Shaw who quipped, "God created us in his image, and we decided to return the favor."[43] Don't let the doctor play God for you. He is still just "practicing medicine." There are dangers in quackery, medications, and pronouncing the wrong diagnoses. There are also dangers in doctors who are certain about what they know until they are certain of something else because of reading the latest scientific article.[44] Expect the family doctors' understanding of depression to be partial at best.[45] Don't be the patient who eagerly swallows anything the doctor offers—"be it theories, ideas, philosophies, ethics, or morality." Discriminate about what you learned at the doctor's visit—"take [his information] apart, chew it up, digest it, and really assimilate."[46]

Why is this important when you have had a thorough medical exam? The answer is profound, if not shocking. There is not a definitive test such as an x-ray or blood draw that will show you suffer from situational depression. An MRI or CT scan won't reveal whether you suffer from depression. The

40   Cousens and Mayell, *Depression-Free for Life*, 26.
41   McLeod, *Lifting Depression*, 13.
42   Greenberg, *Manufacturing Depression*, 342.
43   Awbrey, *Finding Hope in the Age of Melancholy*, 116.
44   Gary Kaplan and Donna Beech, *Total Recovery: Solving the Mystery of Chronic Pain and Depression* (New York City: Rodale Publishers, 2014), 98.
45   See Klein, *From Sad to Glad*, 96.
46   Dayringer, *Dealing with Depression*, 43.

same goes for a urine sample, stool sample, and a culture of your throat. Putting it simply, there is no biochemical test for detecting depression.

The only way a doctor has of determining if you suffer from situational depression is by assessing your symptoms. Symptoms, in this case, are defined as what you exhibit and what you say you have experienced. For instance, one day I looked out the window and asked my husband, "Do you see the wind?" He said, "No, but I see leaves being blown everywhere." The blown leaves are what the doctor evaluates—or, as Antonio said in Shakespeare's *The Merchant of Venice*, "I do not know why I am so sad; it wearies me. You say, it wearies you, but where I found it, came by it, where it is born, I am yet to learn."[47]

The doctor looks for various symptoms. He observes how you are dressed. He is not looking for the expensive outfit or perfectly coiffed hair. He is noticing whether you are neat and well-groomed. He will observe how you sit down. Do you have perfect posture when you sit or do you slump over? He will also observe if you sigh or exhale when you speak, which is a symptom of depression. Then comes his questions. Each question fits in a category below—

Mood.

Are you down on yourself? Does your spouse refer to you as "a wet blanket"? Do you have low self-esteem? Are you interested in social activities or hobbies? Are you frequently irritable and angry?

Energy loss.

Do you feel exhausted after a good night's sleep? How many naps do you take on a typical day? Do you struggle with staying awake?

---

47   Dayringer, *Dealing with Depression*, 29.

Concentration.

Do you react to what others say or do? Do you overreact at the slightest criticism? Has your ability to think and concentrate been slowed down?

Changes in appetite.

Is your appetite excessive? Do you eat a regular meal, or do you have personal restrictions?

Suicidal thoughts.

Do you wish you were dead? Have you plotted out ways to take your life?

Change in sleep patterns.

Do you sleep more than seven hours a night? Do you struggle to fall asleep and stay asleep?

Hopelessness and helplessness.

Do you have feelings of hopelessness? Do you feel successful in your life's journey?

Loss of pleasure – avoidance of pleasant thoughts.

Do you have trouble remembering or imagining pleasant thoughts?

Indecision.

Is it difficult to make a decision even about simple matters?

The doctor may request that you respond to a questionnaire or a battery of forms that rate your life enjoyment and satisfaction, such as the Quick Inventory of Depressive Symptomatology. He may prefer the Ryff Well-Being Scale, which measures your emotional state by asking you to rate on a scale of one to six whether you agree with statements, such as "For me, life has been a continuous process of learning, changing, and growth" or "My daily activities often seem trivial and unimportant."[48]

After observing, asking you questions, and perhaps administering a written test, the family doctor will suggest that you are probably suffering from some form of depression.

But what kind of depression?

Depressive disorders vary. Sometimes what the patient is experiencing and calling depression is just discouragement. For example, "A thirty-three-year-old woman who was not able to bear children [had] a telephone call from an adoption agency informing her that she was about to be a mother to a three-year-old Asian-American. 'I was so excited I couldn't remember my husband's telephone number at work. But I got a hold of him and told him that he was a father. He was so choked up that he couldn't talk.'"[49] Or look at this example: "A sixty-six-year-old widower with a twinkle in his eye recalled how he had met a new friend at church: 'She smiled at me from across the aisle. It sure surprised me. She looked beautiful and I reckoned that she was about my age. I took a shine to her immediately!'"[50] The doctor could pronounce these patients cured, but it really isn't necessary. The gleeful patients are already walking out of the office.

The doctor may pronounce the depression mild or situational and assure the patient it will go away by itself—no treatment necessary. This is the best scenario and the best outcome from the doctor's visit.

For all other descriptions of depression, be assured the doctor won't give the same advice as Lucy in the *Peanuts* comic strip, although it isn't that bad: "I have deep feelings of

---

48   Greenberg, *Manufacturing Depression*, 129.
49   Veninga, *Gift of Hope*, 33.
50   Veninga, *Gift of Hope*, 33.

depression," Charlie Brown said. "What can I do about it?" Lucy advised, "Snap out of it."[51] Nor do I think the doctor will tell you, "Pull yourself together," "Buck up," "Take it like a man," "Don't be a wimp," or "Be strong."

Instead of these trite sayings, the doctor will give you a sophisticated label. You don't need to own the label. Labels are for canned tomatoes, soups, or pickles, not for you. Labels serve a tentative, although helpful function for the doctor and your insurance provider, but can be devastating to you.[52] Labels are part of the American Psychiatric Association's *Diagnostic and Statistical Manual of Mental Disorders* (DSM). The *DSM* is a compendium of psychological troubles sorted into groups; from there, troubles are sorted into individual diagnoses, such as major depressive disorder or manic-depressive disorder. The *DSM* is indispensable to the business of therapy, for it assigns to each diagnosis a five-digit code. Written on a bill, the code unlocks "insurance treasuries, guaranteeing that therapists are treating a disease rather than, say, just sitting around and talking to people about what matters to them."[53] The *DSM* sits on the shelf of virtually every therapist in the nation, including me.

The following are some of the labels or diagnoses accepted by the American Psychiatric Association and insurance companies—

Chronic Depression.

This label means that the doctor has observed that your feelings of depression are intense enough to disrupt all aspects of your life, including everyday activities such as eating, sleeping, and relaxing.[54]

---

51   Aguirre, *Depression: Biographies of Disease*, 142.
52   Gilbert, *Pastoral Care of Depression*, 33.
53   Greenberg, *Manufacturing Depression*, 14–15.
54   Cousens and Mayell, *Depression-Free for Life*, 23.

Manic Depression.

This label means that the doctor has observed cycles of elevated highs and extreme lows. Such mood swings are often referred to as a bipolar disorder.

Biochemical Imbalance.

Although not a clinical label, the term is bandied about by doctors to indicate an imbalance of chemicals in the body.

Seasonal Affective Disorder.

This label suggests that winter is not your season. The blues are common in climates where there is little sunshine.

Postpartum Depression.

This label is for women only. It is depression suffered by women after the birth of a child.

No matter the label, whether the depressed patient admits it or not, all patients without exception hope there is a doctor, an herbalist, or some medically trained practitioner who can help. No patient wants to be stuck in depression the rest of his or her life.[55] When your car battery dies and you are stranded or stuck on the highway at night, just knowing that a mechanic is on his way brings immediate relief. Similarly, just knowing a doctor will suggest treatment brings relief.

No patient enters a doctor's office just wanting to know what the problem is and to get a label for that problem. Every patient wants the doctor to treat and solve the problem.

---

55   McLeod, *Lifting Depression*, 40.

Treatment

What you want is full recovery from depression, not just an improvement of your symptoms. It is no secret that your body has self-healing capacities. Got a paper cut? Apply Neosporin and a Band-aid, and by tomorrow it's all better. Have a headache? Take an aspirin. Have heartburn? Try Tums. Can't sleep? Swallow an Excedrin PM. If you listen to pharmaceutical advertisements long enough, you will discover there's a remedy for nearly every physical malady. If this were really true or even partially true, wouldn't it seem inconsistent that your psyche is the only part of your body that "does not possess regenerative and restorative powers"?[56]

Of course, the psyche has regenerative powers just like your physical body. If not, why would the family doctor or any other medical practitioner prescribe a treatment for depression? The question the doctor faces is not whether to prescribe treatment but rather which treatment has the greatest probability of helping you.

Each family doctor, no matter where he received his medical degree or how long she has been in practice, fishes in

---

56   Kline, *From Sad to Glad*, 174.

the same pool of knowledge in search of the best treatment for depression.[57] The search is not easy, because a doctor has to slog through scientific journals and the same advertisements that you do—and more. He needs to be smart enough and wise enough to find reliable information and offer advice that is helpful. She can't simply offer a health fad du jour, a risky proposition, or a dubious product that will soon meet the same fate as the Edsel. Take, for instance, the medicine salesman of the early 1900s—

> [The] salesman came through town and parked his wagon in the middle of the dusty main street. He stood on the back of the wagon. People gathered around to hear what he had to say, and soon there was a large crowd. The salesman's pitch became more and more impassioned. Soon he worked the crowd into a frenzy. He promised them that his brand of medicine would cure dysentery, consumption (tuberculosis), arthritis, and even reverse the ravages of old age. And, to prove his point further, he added, "What I'm telling you is the gospel truth. But don't just believe me. Look right here. It's written right here on the bottle."[58]

Although the itinerant salesman is a product of yesteryear and has gone the way of the horse and buggy, false curative claims for medical products are still problematic today. Ever read the small print on medical advertisements of the cure-all product? I quote: "Side effects may include nausea, vomiting, rectal dysfunction, and death." Yet marketers and pharmaceutical companies, out to make more than a buck, promote their "health-restorative products" as highly effective. Their advertisements reach tens of millions of viewers on

---

57 Dayringer, *Dealing with Depression*, xvii.
58 McLeod, *Lifting Depression*, 42–43.

television, infomercials, and the internet, and their sales representatives regularly make office calls to your doctor.[59]

Believe me, your doctor prefers a "one-size-fits-all" treatment for his patients with situational depression. But such is not the case. The family physician needs more than a hammer in his tool chest and a recognition that every patient with depression is not a nail. He also needs to be cautious in not equating your depression with that of his last patient. Comparing and contrasting doesn't work, because no one comes out the winner.

You've heard the story of the man whose leg was amputated; he emotionally struggled with his terrible loss until he saw a man with both legs amputated. He felt unjustified for feeling bad over his one lost leg until he saw a man who needed only a cane. It was then he felt his loss more keenly. When the two men spoke, the amputee explained that his amputation was due to diabetes. The man with a cane told of a car accident that had caused a minor injury to his back. Still comparing losses, the amputee said, "At least you have two legs." The man with the cane replied, "Yes, I do, but I lost my wife in the accident."

With more than a hammer in his tool chest and seeing you as a unique patient, your doctor will recommend one of the following conventional treatments—

Hospitalization

If the doctor perceives that your depression is out of control, or that you are suicidal, he will recommend hospitalization in a psychiatric unit where a team of medical personnel will closely evaluate you. The mere fact that your doctor listened and suggested a short stint in a hospital will confirm your suspicions that you need round-the-clock help. Like being

---

59   McLeod, *Lifting Depression*, 43.

prescribed an antibiotic, just knowing that hospital personnel will care for you will bring a sense of relief.[60]

The hospital environment will not be relaxing. It is not like going to a spa or an all-inclusive hotel with waterslides and poolside waiters. Bed rest won't heal your depression, and hospital personnel know that. Television will be kept to a minimum; so will visitors, for you will be too busy to be disturbed. There are group therapy sessions to attend followed by individual therapy, blood draws, and discussions with social workers, a psychiatrist, your family doctor, and other medical personnel too numerous to name. Nurses will make sure that scheduled exercise and eating times are not ignored. You will be given tasks that are boring, monotonous, and menial, such as tooling a belt, coloring in small squares, and putting stickers on a page.

When the pace, exercises, menial tasks, and cafeteria food become annoying, you are turning the corner. You will feel irritated, critical of the nursing staff, and anxious to leave the sterile hospital environment. Believe me, hospital personnel are just as anxious to have you leave.

What you are now experiencing is not a full recovery from depression but a desire to take charge of some phases in your life. It is a desire to get up in the morning when you choose, eat the food you want, exercise at your pace, and select your own hobby. When you want the freedom to choose, medical personnel have succeeded in helping you see the worth in tomorrow. You may not leave the hospital resolute about wanting to fill that tomorrow with newness, but you will leave more resilient than when you checked in. The battle of depression isn't over, but now you have the upper hand. There will be follow-up appointments and questions about resilience to answer another day.

---

60   McLeod, *Lifting Depression*, 43.

Prescription Drugs

It was not until the 1960s that effective antidepressant medications became available for public consumption in spite of strong resistance from the psychoanalytical community. The community viewed antidepressant medication as a Band-aid that covered symptoms of depression while depriving the depressed patient from working through the unconscious conflicts that led to depression.[61] Today, most psychologists see value in prescription drugs and won't hesitate to support antidepressants in conjunction with therapy.

Your family doctor has more than a variety of psychological drugs from which to choose. In fact, he has a whole family of antidepressant drugs at his disposal. For many years Valium, Prozac, and Lithium were the most prescribed antidepressant drugs. Wellbutrin and Mirtazapine are more in vogue today. Whatever the name of the antidepressant drug, there is no single drug—whether natural herb or synthetic—that has proven to be the magic bullet that will alleviate depression. There is no doctor who can confidently say, "Swallow this and your depression will vanish in the wink of an eye, if not a week." If this were the case, such a pill would "lend credence to the belief that biochemical imbalance" is the sole reason for depression.[62]

Since the magic bullet is yet to be discovered, treating depression with an antidepressant drug is not effective in alleviating depression, but it is effective in alleviating some symptoms of depression. In spite of the flaws in antidepressant drugs, a recent survey reveals that one out of three doctor visits by women includes a prescription for an antidepressant drug. Doctors prescribe the drug knowing that there is no guarantee the drug will cure depression.[63]

---

61   Nada L. Stotland, "Recovery from Depression," in David L. Mintz, ed., *Psychiatric Clinics of North America 35*, no. 1 (March 2012): 37–47.
62   Cousens and Mayell, *Depression-Free Life*, 221.
63   Leventhal and Martell, *The Myth of Depression as Disease*, 135.

To say that America has a love affair with antidepressants is not far from the truth. Today there is an "unprecedented epidemic of psychoactive drug use" in our nation. Use of potent, mind-altering conventional drugs is so widespread that it is estimated that Americans consume more than five billon tranquilizers per year.[64]

Taking a pill to alter "the body chemistry is a delicate procedure, not to be undertaken lightly."[65] Your family physician has the power to name your pain and through a pharmacy "dispense your cure one pill at a time."[66] In Aldous Huxley's *Brave New World*, whenever people felt something unpleasant, they took the fictional drug *soma*, "which relieve[d] anxiety and enable[d] them to remain blissfully unaware of old age, death, or anything else that might disrupt their carefully programmed lives."[67] Is this the way you want to live? Some days you might feel that way, but when given the long-term choice I think not.

When your family doctor eagerly says, "I've got a pill that will cure your depression," be cautious.[68] When patients hesitate or refuse to take mind-altering medication, doctors often compare a patient suffering from diabetes with a patient experiencing depression: "Just like diabetics need to take insulin, people who have depression need to take medication."[69]

Despite advances in psychopharmacology, depression is masked, not eradicated, by psychological drugs. But I grant you, the difficult emotional suffering is lessened.[70]

---

64   Cousens and Mayell, *Depression-Free Life*, 21.

65   Kline, *From Sad to Glad*, 12.

66   Greenberg, *Manufacturing Depression*, 24.

67   Awbrey, *Finding Hope in the Age of Melancholy*, 132.

68   Kaplin and Beech, *Total Recovery*, 137.

69   Leventhal and Martell, *The Myth of Depression as Disease*, 32.

70   David L. Mintz and David F. Flynn, "How (Not What) to Prescribe: Non-pharmacological Aspects of Psychopharmacology," in David L. Mintz, ed., *Psychiatric Clinics of North America 35*, no. 1 (March 2012): 158.

Psychotherapy

The famed novelist Stanley Elkin wrote, "Life is either mostly adventure or it's mostly psychology. If you have enough of the one then you don't need a lot of the other."[71]

The unconscious—the interior world that was once the realm of philosophers and priests—has been unlocked by scientific scholars. The father of psychoanalysis, Sigmund Freud, put it this way: "Poets and philosophers before me discovered the unconscious; what I discovered was the scientific method by which the unconscious can be studied."[72] As the voice of mystery in the spoken and unspoken words opens wide for psychologists to observe, it was Baruch Spinoza who said, "I have striven not to laugh at human activities, not to weep at them, not to hate them, but to understand them."[73]

You will find your therapy sessions filled with trial and error (just like the search for the right antidepressant drug) whether your therapist leans heavily on past psychological techniques like Gestalt therapy, transactional analysis, or behavior therapy; past practitioners like Rogers, Skinner, and Ellis; or a host of emerging leaders in psychology like John Gottman, Marsha Lineham, Susan Johnson, or Francine Shapiro. Should you continue in therapy? If the technique the psychologist uses makes a positive difference for you, don't miss a session. If you are asked too many times "How do you feel about . . ," cancel your next appointment. A joke comes to mind—A non-directive therapist on the fourteenth floor of an office building stuck his head out the window and said to the patient who had just thrown himself out, "You feel like killing yourself?"[74]

---

71   Greenberg, *Manufacturing Depression*, 110.
72   Sigmund Freud, quoted in Norman G. Brown, *Life Against Death: The Psychoanalytical Meaning of History* (Middletown, Connecticut: Wesleyan University Press, 1959), 62.
73   Veninga, *Gift of Hope*, 42.
74   Dayringer, *Dealing with Depression*, 21.

It is well known that depressed persons seek help through psychotherapy because they cling to the hope that their depression can be overcome. Typically, the person has exhausted other options and views his problem as unsolvable and insurmountable. "I can't help the way I feel" is a typical response at the first therapy session. Another is, "I cannot control my emotional reactions."

From the days of Epictetus and perhaps before, men have been disturbed not by things, but by the views they take of those things. A depressed person distorts perceptions of self, world, and future in a negative direction. As such, the depressed person is prone to conclude incorrectly or prematurely that she is a failure or a bad person. If life's situations are intolerably harsh and painful, she concludes that her personal world is unfair. If she believes there are no remedies for her depression, she condemns the future.

Are her conclusions correct? By way of a metaphor, if you change the number of votes in a few key swing states by marginal percentage points in a United States presidential election, you dramatically change the direction of the country. The same is true with perception.[75] If you change only a few perceptions, you can dramatically change your depressive mood. Ever had the occasion to say, "Oh, now I see—now I get it." What you were doing was changing your perception.

Unfortunately, we live in a society that expects instantaneous results and gratification. More than a five-minute wait for a burger at McDonald's is too long. A traffic jam of more than two minutes is too long. A patient admitted to a hospital for major surgery and asked to stay more than two days is too long. As with a drive through McDonald's, a traffic jam, or a major surgery, most clients expect to feel better after one or two therapy sessions. It is as if the client is acknowledging that change from depression is necessary

---

75   Korb, *Upward Spiral*, 14.

but knowing and understanding what caused the depression is a luxury. The patient says, "I don't have time for or care to find out."

Not so! You do care! Think about the father whose son yells at him for not letting him borrow the car and tells him he is a bad father—but for whom the yelling and negative assessment bounces off like rain. The only emotion the father feels is love for his son. That's not easy unless you have a good psychologist, who, "like an ancient forest that is choking itself to death, they have to tear out the underbrush . . . and give room for new growth."[76] In other words, you need to learn to see a glass half-full instead of half-empty.

Changing your perception, attitude, and thought will help you better deal with symptoms of depression.[77] Simply put, "The goal of therapy is the systematic unlearning (extinction) of behaviors" that cause symptoms of depression.[78] In psychology this is called a *paradigm shift*. Although the term has become a cliché to describe everything from new hair colors for women to the latest scientific research in physics, the word *paradigm* is still helpful in explaining how change in thinking occurs.[79]

Try this scenario—if you were planning to take a trip by car and had to choose between driving on an interstate or driving on county roads, which would you choose? Most likely you would take the interstate, quickly pull to the left lane, and go five miles per hour over the speed limit. You would stop only on a need basis—to go to the bathroom, gas up the car, or maybe buy a snack. If you did stop for food, it wouldn't be a fancy restaurant where you had to wait to be served. Wendy's or Arby's would do. What would you remember from the trip? You'd remember cars that passed you going fifteen miles over

---

76   Awbrey, *Finding Hope in the Age of Melancholy,* 46.
77   Gilbert, *Pastoral Care of Depression,* 52.
78   Ibid.
79   Awbrey, *Finding Hope in the Age of Melancholy,* 94.

the speed limit and eighteen-wheel trucks that moved into the left lane and forced you to slow down.

That is not how psychotherapy works. If you are the client in a psychotherapy session, you will learn much about traveling on county roads. Such traveling means slowly driving past red barns, cows in the meadow, and farmers cutting hay. It is to pause and see new leaves sprouting on the trees and to gaze at the sunset.[80]

Due to the slower pace of therapy sessions, they are not for everyone with situational depression. But changing the paradigm of situational depression *is* for everyone.

In a sense, the psychologist rents himself out by the hour. As the clock ticks down, so does your session. For the therapist, his time with you is a delicate balance between stepping into your world in search of understanding, then stepping out to convey that understanding to you. How will you know that the therapy sessions are helping? Your depressive symptoms will lessen. Before you leave each session, you will be asked to follow through on a few items discussed. You will also be promised that more help is coming your way at the next session, as if the therapist is dangling a carrot in front of you to make sure that you show up at the next appointment.[81]

But at some point, the therapy sessions will end. More often than not, third-party insurance companies are reluctant to support further treatment when the psychologist acknowledges that symptoms have improved.[82] My favorite joke about sessions ending is, "After ten years in therapy, Sally's psychologist told her something very touching. He said, 'No hablo Ingles.'"[83]

Are your depressive symptoms a thing of the past? Perhaps not, but the sessions are. What should you do now? For the man

80   McLeod, *Lifting Depression*, 25.
81   Greenberg, *Manufacturing Depression*, 225.
82   Nada L. Stotland, "Recovery from Depression," *Psychiatric Clinics of North America 35*, no. 1 (March 2012): 43.
83   Aquirre, *Depression: Biographies of Disease*, 97.

who was still feeling depressed and somewhat suicidal, the psychologist's answer was "Pay your bill today."[84]

Drug and Therapy Treatment

Family physicians often recommend a combination of treatments—medication and psychotherapy. As far as combining treatments is concerned, I don't believe that breakthroughs in drug therapy render techniques of psychotherapy obsolete.[85]

Other Options for the Family Doctor

Hospitalization, prescription drugs, psychoanalytical therapy, and a combination of antidepressant drugs and therapy are the conventional methods for helping the depressed, but there are other methods available to your family doctor. He will no doubt hand you a pamphlet that outlines his version of ways to lessen depression. None of his ideas will be harmful or expensive.

Let me be perfectly clear about one thing: your doctor will never recommend alcohol or drugs as a form of self-medication. Alcoholics are not self-medicating, they are destroying their very lives. Their crippling addiction increases their risk of death.[86] The mortality rate among treated and untreated alcoholics is nearly "three times higher than the general population."[87]

The question is often asked which came first—alcoholism or depression? Although the question is much like the question about the chicken and the egg, in this case the answer is known. Untreated depression does lead to self-medication with alcohol

---

84   Aquirre, *Depression: Biographies of Disease*, 98.

85   Kline, *From Sad to Glad*, 79.

86   Peter Bongiorno, *Holistic Solutions for Anxiety & Depression: Combining Natural Remedies with Conventional Care* (New York: W. W. Norton & Company, 2015), 5.

87   Cousens and Mayell, *Depression-Free Life*, 223.

and drugs. The alcoholic is one of the most tragic and trapped figures in our society. Few have the courage to stop drinking, face the reality of their situation squarely, and say, "In the midst of winter, I finally learned there was in me an invincible summer."[88]

Although the doctor will not recommend alcohol, he may suggest over-the-counter products like St. John's Wart or Vitamin B12.

Don't expect your doctor to be enthusiastic about products sold by zealots in pyramid-type schemes that promise notable changes in depression within a week. He may express a strong bias against zealot salesmen who sound too much like the nineteenth-century salesmen with their cure-all products. Take, for example, my neighbor. In the course of my husband's bout with cancer, I must have looked too frantic, because more than one zealot with a questionable curative product found me. When my husband was within three weeks of his death, a neighbor came rushing over with a drink that promised to cure his cancer for only $180 a month. I tearfully told my neighbor that the cancer had spread throughout his body and doctors at the Huntsman Cancer Center had given him only days to live, but she wouldn't back down from her claims. My husband certainly wasn't the one who would benefit from my buying her product.

Be cautious as you search for help outside of conventional methods. There is merit in exercise and diet and perhaps in adding certain nutrients and supplements to your diet, but don't swallow every hype. Be selective and rational as you search the internet.

Last, but certainly not least, the family doctor may suggest self-help literature. This is where I come in. My competition is fierce, with amazon.com boasting more than seven thousand book titles about happiness and self-help that promise "quick-

---

88   Veninga, *Gift of Hope*, 1.

and-easy paths to lasting happiness."[89] In addition, every day popular media churns out slivers of advice on how to lead a non-depressive life. From Ellen to Dr. Phil, television viewers hear what and what not to eat, how to improve sex life, and the richest source of antioxidants to ward off inflammation.

Within one or two hours, you can know it all, but what have you really learned? Rich or poor, famous or infamous, none are immune from the ravages of depression. You have also learned that no drug, therapy or food group holds the key to unraveling depression. But what you also learned is perhaps there are products like the pieces of a puzzle that can help you.

I don't claim to know it all or expect that my self-help book will be a national bestseller or even a blockbuster. What I do know is that too many friends have confided in me that they suffer from some type of depression. I have stood back and watched them ruin their lives too long, believing that there were better psychologists than me who could help. I have seen too many friends mentally opt out of life and wallow in depression knowing I had the training and talent but did not step forward to help. I can no longer be an observer of such sadness and hold back. Call it compassion or responsibility, it is my hope that readers will not close the book at this juncture.

---

89   Steven Jay Lynn, et al., *Health, Happiness, and Well-Being: Better Living though Psychological Science* (Los Angeles: Sage Publishers, 2015), 251.

CHAPTER SIX

Shrink the Negative

M any people save money in a bank account month after
month for a rainy day. Although the rainy day may never
come, there is security knowing that they have a financial stash.
Others buy food in bulk expecting to ride out a community or
national food shortage. Although the food purchased may go
stale before the crisis hits, they feel secure knowing that they
are prepared for the eventuality. Others amass a wardrobe that
fills more than one closet. These are just a few examples of the
way people gather a reserve.

Just like you might have a financial account, food storage,
and more than one outfit to wear for any occasion, you have
an emotional reserve. But when situational depression rears its
ugly head, you might wonder where that reserve is. It is not
found in the faces of a crowd booing the referee at a basketball
game or in the countenance of the person who stands in line for
concert tickets only to learn that the last ticket sold yesterday.
The reason your emotional reserve is not found in either scenario
is because your reserve never roots in negative expression. It
is deeply rooted in the positive—a sense of gratitude, a happy
remembrance, and a kind gesture.

Unfortunately, the positive is as difficult to hold on to as a butterfly and as slippery as an eel to internalize. The negative, on the other hand, can cling to you like Velcro.[90] Unfortunately, that poses a real problem: a negative expression or reaction to disturbing news magnifies the problem.[91]

This is most clearly demonstrated in the negative thought pattern. For example, those suffering from situational depression often think if A is true then Z is true—and they determine that without considering any of the letters between A and Z. Here are some examples:

A	"My marriage ended in divorce"	→	Z	"I am unlovable. I will never marry again."
A	"I was fired from my job."	→	Z	"No one will ever hire me now."
A	"I didn't pay for the perfume I just put in my purse."	→	Z	"I am a bad person."
A	"Mary is late. She should have been home by now."	→	Z	"Mary is dead."

These kinds of conclusions are imaginative and have no logical or productive basis. Yet the depressed spout such conclusions as facts. I am sure more than one depressed person has been told, "You can make a mountain out of a mole hill" or "It's a gnat, not a flying elephant."

Whether the issue is real or imagined, when situational depression throws you off your game you become good, even expert, at imagining the worst. You can "horriblize" faster

---

90   Alex Korb, *The Upward Spiral: Using Neuroscience to Reverse the Course of Depression. One Small Change at a Time* (Oakland, California: New Harbinger Publications, Inc., 2015), 50.

91   Peter D. Kramer, *Against Depression* (New York City: Viking, 2005), 67.

than Superman can don his cape. You can "catastrophize" quicker than I can blow a bubble. A small disruption in your day's routine is extremely unfortunate. and any mistake—such as adding flour instead of sugar to a recipe—requires self-flagellation. Here's a personal example.

The telephone rang. I picked it up to hear between sobs, "Susan, I'm so sorry."

"Who is this?" I asked. "Are you okay?"

"This is Megan. I didn't sleep all night. I should never had said that to you. I hope you can forgive me. I want to be your friend."

"What are you talking about? I thought we had a great time last night. What did you say?" I literally had no idea.

Pay particular attention to your self-critical thoughts. Are they real or imagined? Can you learn to incorporate the chess model in your thought pattern? At a championship chess match, silence reigns as two players stare at the chess board and occasionally at each other. Each player knows that his opponent has a limited time to make his move, and there's a good reason for that. It's not so the game will end sooner. It's because time matters. If chess players had unlimited time to think, they would repeatedly review and ponder their next move to make sure they had carefully thought out and analyzed all possible consequences.[92] Because there is a time limit, a chess player makes his best decision in the time allotted.

Can you do the same? If so, you are beginning to tap into your emotional reserve and gain control of your emotions. By setting time limits to critical thinking, you automatically shrink negative thoughts. The following are examples—

---

92   Julie A. Fast and John D. Preston, *Get It Done When You're Depressed: 50 Strategies for Keeping Your Life on Track* (New York City: Alpha Books, 2008), 83.

....

At age fourteen, Jennifer committed suicide. Although five years had passed since her death, the tragedy was like yesterday to her mother. Her mother lay in bed most of the day and thought about what she could have done to prevent her daughter's suicide. A psychologist convinced the mother to think about the tragedy but only for one hour a day. The mother decided on two in the afternoon. She set an alarm to remind herself and then got out of bed and functioned throughout the day. When thoughts of Jennifer flooded her mind in the morning, the mother told herself, "I will think about that at two." By so doing, the mother was able to reclaim hours in her day.

....

Tom's secretary stole $60,000 from his firm. When he discovered the theft, he had to adjust to allow for the loss. To pay his employees and not disrupt the flow of business, Tom took out a second mortgage on his home. Although Tom never missed a day of work, he couldn't stop thinking about the theft and what he could have done to prevent it. He was so lost in thought that when asked about his feelings on a merger at the last board meeting, Tom replied, "Could you repeat the question?"

Tom's psychologist suggested that he shrink the negative in his life. He suggested that Tom select half an hour to an hour in the day to think about his secretary and the theft. Tom choose five in the afternoon—the time he was driving home from work. When thoughts of his secretary flooded his mind during the day, he told himself, "I'm saving that for the drive home." By so doing, Tom reclaimed hours in the day and was able to increase his business output.

....

Unlike Jennifer's mother and Tom, thirty-eight-year-old Michel de Montaigne did not set time limits. In 1571, he retired from society to his library tower and spent ten years contemplating and writing. Reflecting on his years in the library tower, de Montaigne wrote, "My life has been full of terrible misfortunes, most of which never happened."[93]

Don't let what happened yesterday or an imagined event that might happen tomorrow rob you of your now or your future. That is easier said than done. The reason for the difficulty is that you have been trained to tune out the present. Have you ever been proud of yourself for being a multitasker? Have you ever found yourself stopped at a traffic light, thinking—

"Did Bill text me? I should check the phone."

"Did John remember to pick up Sammy from school?"

"Did I leave the stove on?"

"Did I remember to pack my thumb drive? I really need visuals for my presentation."

And when the light turns green, the motorist in the car behind you honks because you are not moving forward. Why? You are lost in thought.

Random thoughts moving in and out of the here and now are hard to stop. It is a well-known fact that stopping not just one but hundreds of thoughts from crowding out the present is nearly impossible. A recent study of "5,000 people by psychologists Matthew Killingsworth and Daniel Gilbert of Harvard University, found adults spend only about 50% of their time in the present moment."[94] In other words, you are mentally checked out half of the time.

---

93 Korb, *The Upward Spiral*, 38.
94 Emma Seppala, "Secrets of a Happier Life," *Time* (New York: Time Inc., 2017), 13.

If "checked out" describes you, how do you expect to "live in the moment" and *carpe diem*? How can you expect treatment for situational depression to work when you are looking in the rearview mirror half of the time? Research shows that if you live your life in the present, you will be happier. This has proven true even when you are engaged in a distasteful task like cleaning toilets, paying bills, and taking out the trash.

How can your emotional reserve help you stay in the moment? Remember what you learned in elementary school: "Before you cross the street stop, look, and listen." Apply the stop, look, and listen theory to your thoughts. When your thoughts turn negative, stop. Take a mental look at where such thoughts are leading you. If they are leading you in a downward trajectory, stop. Look and see. Listen and hear your surroundings. Can you hear the bird singing, boys up the street playing ball, or a baby crying? Do you see flowers blooming, a neighbor mowing his lawn, or the church at the end of the street? In other words, bring your mind back to the present.

Just like instinctively recoiling when you see a slithering snake or pulling your hand quickly away from a hot pan on the stove, pull back from negative thoughts.[95] You don't have to go over the unhappy incident again and again looking for a hidden or undisclosed meaning. Sigmund Freud, the father of psychology, said it best: "Sometimes a cigar is just a cigar."[96] All that is required of you is to pull back.

I also like an ancient Chinese saying: "You can't stop the birds from flying overhead, but you can stop them from making nests in your hair."[97] The way to keep the birds from nesting is to act. Talking about the issue has merit, but it doesn't take the place of acting.

Stand up, get off the couch, and do more than head to the refrigerator or bathroom. If you still prefer to lounge around,

---

95   Lynn, *Health, Happiness, and Well-Being*, 64.
96   Kaplan and Beech, *Total Recovery*, 52.
97   Lynn, *Health, Happiness, and Well-Being*, 42.

don't think you are safe and can hide for long. Consider an experience that happened to me—

On a gloomy Monday when I was a young mother with two children and pregnant with my third, no amount of coaxing from my children could get me out of bed. Life had thrown me one too many curve balls, and a morning of wallowing in self-pity was long overdue.

When the doorbell rang, I said to my sons, "Let's pretend we're not home. Be real quiet." Sensing a possible game, my sons complied. The doorbell rang again and again but we did not go to the door.

"Susan, I know you are in there. Let me in," shouted Jane.

"Go away," I shouted back. "I want to be left alone."

I'm still not sure what Jane's occupation was before she moved into my neighborhood, but she knew how to pick the lock on my sliding glass door with her credit card. As she entered my home, I could hear her talking to herself as she walked toward my bedroom: "What a mess! How can anyone live like this! Cheerios are matted in the carpet, dirty diapers laying on the floor, flies, and the dishes look like they haven't been washed for a week."

At that moment, I really disliked Jane. Before I had a chance to feel hatred towards her, she threw open the bedroom door, looked at me, and said, "You've never looked worse."

Then she did something that changed my life. Jane grabbed me by the hand and said, "Let's get going." She didn't say, "*You* need to get going." She said, "*Let's* get going."

Jane pulled me out of bed and we went to work. It was a busy morning washing the dishes, vacuuming the carpet, polishing the furniture, and washing and drying the sheets. Jane did most of the work while I picked up the clutter. She even fixed lunch for my family.

As Jane and I sat at the kitchen table, she asked, "What are you going to do now?"

"Since I have clean sheets, I'm going back to bed," I said.

"Oh, no you're not!" replied Jane.

There was silence until Jane asked, "What do you think your talent is? What are you good at?

"Nothing."

Jane looked at the piano in the corner of the room and said, "You can play the piano. That's not nothing."

She got up from the table and reached for the phone. She telephoned a piano teacher in our ward. I overheard her say, "Susan wants to come to your house tomorrow for a piano lesson. What time is best for you? Ten o'clock will be fine. By the way, I'll pay for her first lesson."

"You'd better not go back to bed," Jane said as she was walking out the door. "You need to practice the piano; otherwise, you're going to be really embarrassed. The piano teacher is a gossip."

I did practice that day and the next morning before showing up for the piano lesson. What I played for the teacher is not important, but what the teacher said was: "That was interesting." Her comment said to me, "You'll never be a great pianist."

Looking back on that episode in my life, I am confident that I was never meant to be a concert pianist. I am just as confident that I will always be grateful for my friend Jane. What Jane knew on that gloomy Monday was that I was not meant to spend that day or the next wallowing in self-pity. The same goes for you.

If you are still saying, "Not today; perhaps tomorrow I'll get off the couch," you are deciding to remain inactive—to let the world pass by. Inactivity doesn't work any better than negative thoughts, no matter how you slice it.

Get up! Even if your standing up borders on "baby steps" like Bill Murray in *What about Bob*, get up! If you make mistakes in the morning or afternoon, keep moving, because "if you're making mistakes, it means you're out there doing something."[98] What you are doing is tapping into emotional reserves and shrinking the negative in your life.

---

98   Korb, *The Upward Spiral*, 128.

CHAPTER SEVEN

Emotional First-Aid

If you have been in a terrible car accident and a stranger comes on the scene, he will do more than call 911. He will check your pulse, make sure you are breathing, put a tourniquet around a bleeding leg, and try to keep you warm and calm. The stranger will stay with you until the ambulance arrives to transport you to a hospital, where surgery will be performed if needed. If the accident is not horrific, the stranger's first-aid assistance will be all that is needed.

Too often people who suffer from situational depression demand surgery to solve their problem when all that is needed is first-aid. Take the case of Kathy. She didn't want any anti-depressant pills if they couldn't provide immediate relief. She didn't want therapy sessions once a week. Kathy wanted the therapist at her beck and call day and night. Why? She had tried everything to solve her problem, and in the process of retelling her shocking experience she exhausted herself as well as her neighbors, friends, and family members. Kathy's concluding remark to medical practitioners regarding the event that derailed her world is the familiar refrain, "I've tried everything."

What Kathy is really saying is that she has tried everything in her "logical class," which means she has sifted through her pot of knowledge, habits, and background data and has found nothing that can solve her problem. Kathy no longer thinks that if she tried another one hundred times to solve the problem using the same logical class, she will find the answer.

What Kathy has failed to do is "think outside the box"—find a resolution outside the realm of the ordinary. Before she succumbs to full-blown depression, she needs emotional first-aid—an adjustment or course correction to maintain a positive, healthy, even exuberant love for life.

Emotional first-aids are not meant to consume your day or even a large portion of your day. They are meant to brighten your day—to shrink the negative. Give these aids a genuine try instead of just giving them lip service. Try one, try five, or try them all. They are presented in alphabetical order, not in order of importance. After all, if I had placed diet and exercise first, would you really keep reading?

Eye Blinking.

When you are not focused on the here and now, you do not blink your eyelids as often. The quickest and easiest way to bring your thoughts back to the present is to blink your eyelids rapidly. Try it. If you are having a negative thought blink, and then blink again.

Clutter.

When in doubt, through throw it out. Magazines, newspapers, and even grandma's antique flower vases may have to go. Look around your home and decide what is essential and what takes up space but does not hold the value it once did. When you rid yourself of clutter, depressive thoughts dissipate.

Creativity.

Create! Create! Create some more! Use color in a new way. Rearrange the pictures in your bedroom. Why? Artistic creativity is one of the first things cast aside when situational depression hits. "It's as though your eye for color and design disappear. Ideas dry up, and your usually active and creative mind becomes static."[99] Reawaken the creativity that has taken a backseat to what you have presumed were "more important tasks," like the business of life.

Perhaps yesterday you thought of sitting down and playing the piano but pushed aside the self-indulgent thought because of dishes in the sink and dirty floors in the kitchen. That was yesterday, not today. You need a creative outlet. The passion and intensity inherent in creativity are powerful antidotes to fight situational depression. And here's another fact worth remembering: "the act of creation, whether it be at the highest level of artistic endeavor or expressed at more mundane everyday levels, can bolster your self-esteem and connect you to your highest self."[100]

You may not compose like Mozart or direct the Tabernacle Choir on Temple Square like Mack Wilberg, but the creative process will heighten your mood "regardless of the commercial appeal or artistic merit of the final product."[101]

Diet.

No one likes pizza or chocolate better than me. But a diet of pizza and chocolate every day for dinner will do me little good. It's not just the weight gain that will be problematic. Scientific research strongly suggests that "aspects of mood and behavior [are] affected by the foods we eat and by the nutritional

99   Fast and Preston, *Get It Done When You're Depressed*, 243.
100   Cousens and Mayell, *Depression-Free for Life*, 208.
101   Ibid.

supplements we take or fail to take."[102] Ever thought of going on a "diet low in whatever tastes sweet?"[103] Neither have I, but there is a correlation between increased intake of sugar and depression that you may want to consider the next time you shop for junk food or that tasty midnight snack.

Exercise.

Sitting is the new smoking. "If it weren't for the fact that the TV set and the refrigerator are so far apart," joked comedian Joey Adams, "some of us wouldn't get any exercise at all."[104] Research studies show that people who take an "occasional walk live longer and happier lives than those who are sedentary."[105] Studies also show that if you are physically fit, you have a better chance of weathering the storm clouds of situational depression.

The exercise you choose doesn't have to be intense or aerobic to benefit your mood.[106] For example, unwrap the Fitbit you got for Christmas, strap it to your arm, and start walking. Doctors recommend 10,000 steps a day. How can you walk that many steps in a day? Take the stairs for anything less than three floors. Walk to do errands that are less than a mile away. Don't take an escalator if stairs are nearby.[107] Stop circling the parking lot for the better space; take the first parking space you see and then walk the distance.

If you tend grandchildren or take the dog out for an evening stroll, it may not feel like exercising, but your steps are adding up. If you're a homeowner, there are plenty of opportunities to stay active year-round without ever joining a fitness center. Want a whole-body workout? Rake the leaves, shovel the snow,

---

102 Cousens and Mayell, *Depression-Free for Life*, 4.
103 Malcolm Noell McLeod, *Lifting Depression: The Chromium Connection* (Laguna Beach, California: Basic Health Publications, Inc., 2005), 21.
104 Lynn, *Health, Happiness, and Well-Being*, 223.
105 Cousens and Mayell, *Depression-Free for Life*, 204.
106 Cousens and Mayell, *Depression-Free for Life*, 202.
107 Korb, *The Upward Spiral*, 91.

sweep the sidewalk, or prune the bushes. Chop vegetables, knead bread, clean the stove, vacuum the carpet—you know the routine. The message is *move*. You won't get a runner's high from the extra steps, but you'll feel exhilarated when the Fitbit displays fireworks in celebration of your achievement.

Gardening.

There is nothing like playing in the dirt—remember the fun you had digging in a sandbox and building castles on the beach years ago? Plant flowers, mow the lawn, pull weeds, or trim a tree. If you don't have the opportunity to garden, purchase a houseplant. Studies show even a houseplant can be "quite calming."[108]

Heat.

If you are inside and feeling depressed, turn down the thermostat. Don't reach for a sweater, mittens, scarf, or electric blanket. If you are cold enough to shake, you won't feel depressed.

Hormonal Changes.

No doubt, you've heard of pre-menstrual blues and postpartum depression. Ask any woman: they are real. Try a simple calendar approach to charting your menstrual cycle. Mark on a calendar when your monthly cycle begins. If a negative situation happens just before your menstrual cycle is scheduled to start, the situation may not be as bad as you think. For example—

> Coming home from a shopping spree at the mall, Maria put on her latest purchase and asked her husband, "How do you like my blue dress?"

---

108 Bongiorno, *Holistic Solutions for Anxiety & Depression*, 50.

"I like it okay," her husband said, glancing up from his devise. "My favorite is still the red dress. The dress I picked out for you."

Maria became visibly upset and screamed, "You never like anything I choose." She ran to the bedroom, slammed the door behind her, fell on the bed, and cried.

If the same situation had occurred later in the month, Maria might have responded, "I like the red dress, too, but this one was on sale and I think it works." The husband would have looked up from his devise and said, "It does work. You look beautiful."

It's a good idea to let people in your household know that on certain days you are sensitive to comments. The mere fact that many women experience depression at specific times in their reproductive cycle suggests a strong correlation between the role of estrogen or other hormonal replacements and depression.[109]

IQ.

Often those who are extremely smart, bordering on genius, experience off-the-chart highs and extreme lows. If you are a gifted mathematician, musician, or scholar, be prepared for a rocky ride—but could you imagine life being complete without the intellect that is yours? How could wishy-washy comments like "That's nice" or "That's too bad" fit you? Take life with all its gustoes and detours, and hang on for a wild ride of hopes and dreams intermixed with devastating disappointments. It's just DNA.

---

109 Cousens and Mayell, *Depression-Free for Life*, 54.

Laughter.

In the movie *Mary Poppins,* the actors sang, "I Love to Laugh."

> I love to laugh
> Loud and long and clear
> I love to laugh
> It's getting worse every year
>
> The more I laugh, the more I fill with glee
> And the more the glee
> The more I'm a merrier me, it's embarrassing
> The more I'm a merrier me

The old saying "Laughter is the best medicine" isn't far from the truth. Have you heard this one? "Johnny was always trying to copy my homework. I wonder whatever happened to ol' Johnny Xerox."

Light.

Late at night an inebriated man dropped his car keys in the parking lot. He looked for them in the only area that had a lamppost. A police officer approached him and said, "Hey friend, you could have lost your keys anywhere in this parking lot—why do you only look over here?' The drunk man replied, "Because the light is better."[110]

John Denver sang, "Sunlight on my shoulders makes me happy." While I doubt the famed singer ran a clinical trial on his lyrics, he did have a clear "understanding of sunlight's benefit on mood."[111] Unfortunately, the environment in which you live has devised a sinister scheme to block the sun—inside work, car travel, air pollution, and even sunblock lotion.

---

110 Bongiorno, *Holistic Solutions for Anxiety & Depression,* 116.
111 Bongiorno, *Holistic Solutions for Anxiety & Depression,* 42.

Don't live in a dark house. Walnut furniture is beautiful, but it's another dimension of dark. You may look your best in a black sheath, but not now. Wear that bright pink dress that hangs in the back of your closet or the yellow tie that is too bright for a sedate occasion. Brighten your world.

Look Your Best.

As situational depression takes hold, there is an urge to reach for comfort clothing—sweatshirts, baggy pants, and pajamas—before walling up in your personal cave. In the darkness of the cave, personal grooming is kept to a minimum—no makeup, hair pulled back in a ponytail. You know the look. It doesn't take much effort to look a 2 or 3 on a 10-point scale.

You are about to rejoin society's preoccupation with the multibillion-dollar industry of appearance. I am not suggesting reconstructive cosmetic surgery or support garments, but I am suggesting that you make every effort to look your best. Few women wallow in situational depression when they look a 10 on a 10-point scale. It takes effort to look 10 out of 10 and turn heads wherever you go. Your effort may include scheduling an appointment for a makeover and a new hair style, treating yourself to a pedicure, and shopping for a jaw-dropping outfit.

Music.

Turn up the music! Be more than a listener—sing along, and sing really loud. Clap your hands and move your feet. Why? You've got rhythm! Push back the furniture and give yourself room to practice your dance moves. Remember the movie *Napoleon Dynamite*? He was shy and picked on until he heard the music and began to dance.

Nature.

Depression doesn't like the great outdoors. Walk around the block. Better yet, walk around two blocks. As beautiful as houses with expansive lawns can be, there is nothing as stunning as trees in their natural habitat, walking into a sunset, or watching the shimmering waves of the ocean.

Posture.

Artists depict the look of depression with a blank stare, downcast eyes, and head supported by a hand. Want to fool depression? Straighten up and hold your head high.

Relaxation Techniques.

Take time to smell the roses. Relaxation techniques help make that possible. Try this simple exercise: When you "find your mind wandering, take a deep breath in; as you breathe out, let go of your thoughts—as if you were consciously exhaling them—and bring your attention back to the present."[112]

Guided imagery or visualization is also effective. See yourself at the ocean. Feel the wind and the surf on your face. Feel the warmth of the sun and hear the sound of seagulls flying overhead.[113]

There is also "systematic and progressive relaxation of different muscle groups."[114] Tense and relax muscles in a progressive manner by starting with your head and ending with your toes.

The expected outcome of focusing on breathing, imagery, and progressive relaxation of muscle groups is "calm yet alert, relaxed yet focused, resting yet awake."[115]

Rubber Band Snapping.

Wear an elastic band on your wrist at all times. Each time you have a negative thought, pull back the rubber band and

---

112 Seppala, "Secrets of a Happier Life," 16.
113 Venega, *A Gift of Hope*, 92.
114 Lynn, *Health, Happiness, and Well-Being*, 156.
115 Cousens and Mayell, *Depression-Free for Life*, 215.

snap it against your wrist.[116] Just like the rubber rebounds, so will you.[117]

Schedule Your Time.

Structure your day and stick to a schedule. Get out of bed by 7 a.m., eat breakfast by 8 a.m., exercise at 9 a.m., and so on. As depression lessons, flexibility will become a welcomed friend.[118]

Shower/Cold.

Once you're over the initial shock of a cold shower, it is invigorating.[119] Cold water elevates your mood immediately.

Sleep.

It was F. Scott Fitzgerald who said, "The worst thing in the world is to try to sleep and not to."[120] Most people need about eight hours of sleep. The older you are, however, the less sleep you need. When you're waiting for a Social Security check to arrive, expect that seven hours will do.[121]

Since you spend about a third of your life asleep (or at least trying to fall asleep), even small changes in sleep patterns will affect your mood.[122] If you've been up all night for whatever reason, you will be "out of sorts" the next day. As a general rule, go to bed before midnight—when it comes to sleep, "one hour before midnight is worth two hours after midnight."[123]

---

116 Dayringer, *Dealing with Depression*, 64.
117 Mandy Oaklander, "How to Bounce Back," *Time* (New York: Time Inc., 2017), 24.
118 Fast and Preston, *Get It Done When You're Depressed*, 33.
119 Bongiorno, *Holistic Solutions for Anxiety & Depression*, 51.
120 Aquirre, *Depression: Biographies of Disease*, 34.
121 Korb, *The Upward Spiral*, 119.
122 Korb, *The Upward Spiral*, 89.
123 Bongiorno, *Holistic Solutions for Anxiety & Depression*, 17.

Technology.

The small bright lights of technology are here to stay. Take advantage of funny videos and audiotapes. Instead of listening to news media as you commute to work, "lighten your mood and boost your health by listening to comedy routines and popular humor books."[124]

Writing Thoughts.

If you struggle with the same thought spinning around and around in your head, write down the thought on a piece of paper. If the recorded thought is worrisome, write one happy memory, also.

And so the list goes. I hope that one, five, or ten of the emotional first-aid measures have piqued your interest. At this very moment you may be laughing, in deep muscle relaxation, dressed in a stunning outfit, eating a carrot, and snapping your wrist with a rubber band.

Although I applaud your efforts, emotional first-aid will not solve situational depression. The good news is that emotional first-aid does mask and lessen symptoms of depression. What I'm trying to say is this: you could eat vegetables, exercise, sing, blink, chart menstrual cycles, and live in a house with the temperature set at fifty-eight degrees, and whatever caused your situational depression will still be present.

Life can be an uphill climb with cold wind in your face, but it doesn't have to be. Emotional first-aid works, but you can't spend the rest of your life depending on first-aid any more than an accident victim can expect a stranger to still be administering artificial respiration long after the victim is breathing on her own.

---

124 Cousens and Mayell, *Depression-Free for Life*, 210.

CHAPTER EIGHT

The Core

"This book is well worth the price," you say. "I'm gardening, swimming, and playing the violin, and best of all, I have no symptoms of depression. Depression is a thing of the past—I've moved on."

Not so fast! When depression begins to lift, you will start to feel like your old self because the time and energy lost on depression has been replaced by first-aid techniques. You aren't through with depression, but you are on the right track.

Michael reported his situational depression had passed after just a few weeks of trying emotional first-aid techniques. He went back to work part-time and, as the saying goes, "time passed." He thought the episode that had turned his world upside down was behind him until a well-meaning friend asked, "How are you?"

It wasn't that others had not asked him the same question a dozen times. His reply—"I'm good," "Fine," "I've moved on"— was not forthcoming this time. The simple question "How are you?" pushed Michael over the edge. It was as if he realized for the first time his son would rather live on the streets than live with him. Michael left work without proffering an excuse, drove directly to his home, and crawled back inside his cave.

This time his depression had no bounds—no walls, windows, ceiling, or floor.

Do I have your attention? As well-intentioned as first-aid measures are in disrupting situational depression, making them part of your everyday life is not enough to ensure depression will not reemerge with vengeance. It's like being stung by a wasp for the first time. Your allergic reaction that causes your arm to swell up like a red balloon can be solved by a simple prescription. The second time you're stung could be fatal if you do not quickly receive medical aid. So before you call *America's Got Talent* to show your new dance moves and before you envision your workout program superseding the Ironman Cowboy's record of fifty ironmen races in fifty states in fifty days, it's time to regroup to ensure you do not fall into a cave like Michael.

The reason why emotional first-aid didn't eradicate Michael's problem is because depression was not solved—it was masked. Does this mean that Michael or you can stop exercising, being creative, or eating healthy food? Absolutely, not! Emotional first-aid techniques will be part of your routine for years to come.

In the years that follow, you will need more than first-aid, however. You need a strong core—meaning you will need people who rush into your life when others rush out. Consider an apple. An apple can last for weeks, perhaps even a month, if the core remains intact. If you cut out the core, the apple will immediately begin to shrivel. Next consider a stone thrown into a placid lake. The stone hitting the water causes ripples to form a circular pattern. If you were the stone, the circles closest to you would be your core. If you were the apple, your core would also be those closest to you.

By way of analogy, the farthest circular ring from the core would be strangers. When you learn of strangers suffering from a flood disaster in Louisiana, you may express sorrow about the flooding over lunch, but in the same sentence you might say, "Please pass the salt and pepper." You are concerned and perhaps may even send monetary relief to Louisiana flood victims, but you are not personally devastated. If you were to learn at lunch that your mother had been trapped by the flood waters while visiting a friend in Louisiana, you would not say, "Pass the salt and pepper." The reason for the different reaction is that your mother is part of your core—she is family.

When I suggested to Michael that his core was family, he threw up his hands and shouted, "My family is the reason I'm talking to you." Although what Michael shouted was true and heartfelt, let's face it—when you wipe away the tears, remove the boxing gloves, and stop to think about what matters most, your family will still top the list. There may be a few elderly or doomsday clients who see a psychologist about the political turmoil in America, the hurricane off the Florida Keys, or the fires in the California mountains, but most clients will have much more to say about family—their core value. Ever wonder why the death of a spouse is so devastating? It is a direct hit to the core. Ever wonder why divorce is so unsettling? It is a direct hit to the core.

No matter what their location or current feelings about each other, family will remain your strongest bond and has been at the core of your social interactions since birth. And right now, you need your family, even with all their warts and imperfections.

"My family abandoned me when I needed them most," Michael yelled. Knowing his story, I'm sure that was the case. Unfortunately, Michael had been "led to believe that when our backs are against the wall, the family becomes cohesive."[125] In my experience that's not necessarily so. The wife you dated, courted, and promised to love and cherish may be the main reason for your depression. Adding to it, she may be totally unsympathetic to your current blues.

---

125 Veninga, *A Gift of Hope*, 30.

As simple as it sounds, "Families can often hurt one another in the days and months following a crisis. Disputes that have been dormant for years erupt to the surface. Battle lines between opposing family factions are formed. Arguments break out over relatively insignificant issues."[126] Before long, the family not only has the crisis to deal with, but the conflicts that too quickly follow in its wake. Take for example the question of which sibling inherits grandma's fine china. The reason family fights are so vicious is because family members know each other's vulnerable spots all too well. And, unfortunately, they know how to stab the knife at the most sensitive nerves.

Under normal circumstances, confidences shared in a family setting would be kept secret. For example, under normal circumstances you would not tease a sister about a weight problem when she had confided in you her anguish at not being asked to prom. You would not chide a brother for lack of ambition after he told you his frustration with a job interview. But a crisis means the family is no longer living in normalcy. Secrets shared in private are ammunition as the battle begins.[127]

My message is simple: When expectations of a loving family understanding and rallying to your side does not materialize, don't give up on family. Just because you expected your wife to throw a big party for your birthday but instead she insisted that a drive-through Taco Bell meal would do, don't reach for the ammunition and start a battle that could escalate into a full-blown war. You "cannot pretend to measure either stress loads or breaking points with the precision an engineer applies to a steel beam," nor can you predict when a hug or intimate embrace could ward off a battle.[128] You have to choose your battles to ensure victory, and there is little victory when the loser is your loved one.

---

126 Veninga, *A Gift of Hope*, 118.
127 Veninga, *A Gift of Hope*, 127.
128 Kline, *From Sad to Glad*, 64.

Insensitivity runs deep in each of us. When Dorothy was in the emergency room waiting to be seen by a doctor, she heard her husband ask his phone, "What time does the BYU game start?" When Bill was waiting in the car for his wife to join him, she went out the back door to visit a neighbor.

Admittedly, it is easier some days to be alone than to interact with family. But did you know that social isolation contributes to lingering depression? Research studies have shown convincingly that "treatments for depression that solely focus on keeping people engaged with others can reduce depression significantly" and "regardless of the type of person they connect with, they consistently felt more upbeat on days when they mingled."[129] And here's another hint—"people with many social connections are less likely to experience sadness, loneliness, low self-esteem, and problems with eating and sleeping."[130]

Your built-in social connection has been and will always be family. Friends may come and go, but family is forever. But with that said, have you ever heard a single parent say, "I couldn't have survived visitation rights without my friend who stood by me, supported me, and gave me a sense of hope"?

If you've ever needed friends other than family, today is the day. You need a friend who will listen and not say, "You'll be okay" or "Let it be," as the Beatles sang. Actor George Burns had such a friend in Jack Benny. Burns said,

> Jack and I had a wonderful friendship for nearly fifty-five years. Jack never walked out on me when I sang a song, and I never walked out on him when he played the violin. We laughed together, we played together, we worked together, we ate together. I suppose that for many of those years we talked every single day.[131]

---

129   Fast and Preston, *Get It Done When You're Depressed*, 158; Ellen Seidman, "Fourteen Ways to Jump for Joy," *Time* (New York: Time Inc., 2017), 40.

130   Carter, *The Sweet Spot*, 117.

131   Veninga, *A Gift of Hope*, 156.

I hope you have such a friend—or, better yet, a handful of such friends. In the movie *Steel Magnolias*, a handful of friends made all the difference. When the vicissitudes of life hit, no matter the extremity, backbiting, or arguments in the past, those friends were there for each other. The University of Chicago's National Opinion Research Center found that "those with five or more close friends are 50% more likely to describe themselves as 'very happy' than those with smaller social circles."[132]

"It is time to make a few phone calls, throw a party, and set up a lunch date," I told Michael. He responded, "When I became depressed, my friends didn't understand, and they stopped texting."

This is when it gets tricky for the psychologist. Michael's hurt is real and an obstacle that can't be brushed aside. Perhaps a story from the life of George Durrant will suggest the next step Michael needs to take:

"Our children had had a restless night....The next morning I had to go to Salt Lake City early. I decided I'd quietly get out of bed and not even wake Marilyn up. I'd just prepare my own breakfast and do everything that needed to be done." When George reached inside his closet for a white shirt, none had been ironed. When he looked for bread to make toast, there was no bread. The hotcakes he made himself were terrible: "With each bite I took I became more and more upset until I was almost beside myself with disgust, frustration, and self-pity."

George banged around the kitchen, but Marilyn didn't wake up. He went to the bedroom closet, got his suit coat, and slammed the closet door. "Out of the corner of my eye I saw Marilyn jump. Now I knew she was awake." George then stormed out of the house without saying goodbye.

---

132   David Futrelle, "Can Money Buy Happiness?" *Time* (New York: Time Inc., 2017), 55.

He stopped at his office to pick up some papers and paused to pray. "As I was praying there was only one thing that I could think about, and that was to ask Heavenly Father to bless my wife Marilyn that she would have a happy day," George wrote. It was then that Heavenly Father put an idea in George's mind. "Why don't you go home and bless her to have a happy day?"

George did go home and said to Marilyn, "I'm sorry. Forgive me."

Making peace with ourselves and others isn't easy. It takes a brave man to admit he's wrong. But as Gandhi said, "The pathway to inner healing is forgiveness."[133]

Forgiveness is not about forgetting, as the old adage would have you suppose. It is about letting go.[134] You may think it is easier to slam the door on family and friends than let go of a hurt or resentment, but it is not. You need people in your life— you need the core. The argument that "it's a cruel world out there" cannot be denied. But there's one argument that trumps sequestering yourself from the cruel world— situational depression will return, and you need a strong core of family and friends who will rush in when others rush out.

It was Barbra Streisand who sang "People" in the 1964 Broadway musical *Funny Girl*:

People who need people,
Are the luckiest people in the world
We're children, needing other children
And yet letting a grown-up pride
Hide all the need inside
Acting more like children than children[135]

---

133 Veninga, *A Gift of Hope*, 39.
134 Carter, *The Sweet Spot*, 170.
135 "People" was composed by Jule Styne with lyrics by Bob Merrill. Recorded December 20, 1963, and released January 1964.

After a lifetime of interacting with those who are depressed in and out of a clinical setting by the bitter cup of non-forgiveness, I stick to my answer—"Let it go!"

Although there are often long processes involved in letting it go, there need not be. Put your hand in the hand of God and step up. Does anyone understand what you've gone through better than the Lord God Omnipotent? He knows you by name and wants you to be happy.

Are you blindsided by the insertion of the Lord in the cure for depression? I hope not. The answer lies in what your Sunday school teacher has said so many times: "The Lord loves you. He's on your side." If you turn to the Lord, you will know Him better and feel his stretched out hand—

> One little girl was drawing a picture with crayons when her teacher walked by and asked her what she was doing. The little girl stated with self-assurance that she was drawing a picture of God. The teacher was amused and taken aback. She told the little girl that no one knows what God looks like, to which the little girl calmly replied: "They will when I am finished."[136]

Although it was the British wit Oscar Wilde who quipped, "When the gods wish to punish us, they answer our prayers," it's not true.[137] It's time to pray and receive comfort and peace. When you get up in the morning, gravity will pull you to your knees. Tell the Lord that you are about to begin a new day, and ask for help to step beyond what appears to be the reality of your life.

After praying comes scripture reading; you know the routine—simple acts of faith. There never seems time enough in any day for the laundry list of "Church dos," but there will be now. Elder L. Whitney Clayton said at the April 2017 General Conference:

---

136 Gilbert, The *Pastoral Care of Depression*, 76.
137 Awbrey, *Finding Hope in the Age of Melancholy*, 36.

A few years ago, I spoke with a young bishop who was spending hours each week counseling with members of his ward. He made a striking observation. The problems that members of his ward faced, he said, were those faced by Church members everywhere—issues such as how to establish a happy marriage; struggles with balancing work, family, and Church duties; challenges with the Word of Wisdom, with employment, or with pornography; or trouble gaining peace about a Church policy or historical question they didn't understand.

His counsel to ward members very often included getting back to simple practices of faith, such as studying the Book of Mormon—as we were counseled by President Thomas S. Monson to do—paying tithing, and serving in the Church with devotion. Frequently, however, their response to him was one of skepticism: "I don't agree with you, Bishop. We all know those are good things to do. We talk about those things all the time in the Church. But I'm not sure you're understanding me. What does doing any of those things have to do with the issues I'm facing?"

It's a fair question. Over time, that young bishop and I have observed that those who are deliberate about doing the "small and simple things"—obeying in seemingly little ways—are blessed with faith and strength that go far beyond the actual acts of obedience themselves and, in fact, may seem totally unrelated to them. It may seem hard to draw a connection between the basic daily acts of obedience and solutions to the big, complicated problems we face. But they are related. In my experience, getting the little daily habits of faith right is the single best way to fortify ourselves against the troubles of life, whatever they may be. Small acts of faith, even when they seem insignificant or entirely disconnected from the specific problems that vex us, bless us in all we do.[138]

The Lord's promise for turning to Him in active devotion is "I, the Lord, am bound when ye do what I say" (D&C 82:10). What is He bound to do? He is bound take you by the hand and lead you to higher ground.

No doubt you're rolling your eyes and saying, this book is a bait-and-switch. The author has lost her psychological focus and no doubt the next story is "Windows of Heaven" starring Lorenzo Snow.

Not so! It was William James, the father of American psychology, who wrote in his *Varieties of Religious Experience* that religion is "to experience union with *something* larger than ourselves and in that union find our greatest peace."[139] If you want peace instead of depression, turn to the Lord. If you want peace and happiness, turn to the Lord, for as noted psychologist Gabriel Cousens wrote, "Overall, people with an appreciation for the spiritual side of life are twice as likely as those with no spiritual connection to consider themselves very happy."[140]

What is the opposite of situational depression? It is hope-filled happiness. Where is it found? Turn to the Lord, cast your burdens upon Him, and wait to see what the Lord has in store for you. Waiting is not synonymous with the wait in the doctor's office, where patients pretend to read mindless drivel about movie stars hoping the nurse will come quickly, call out their name, and put them in a small room where there will be more magazines to browse. Waiting upon the Lord is proactive. It's not sitting on your hands or pacing back and forth in hopes that the wait will soon be over. Waiting upon the Lord is action-packed. It begins with kindness.

---

138 Whitney L. Clayton, "Whatsoever He Saith unto You, Do It," *Ensign*, May 2017.
139 Samuel S. Franklin, *The Psychology of Happiness: A Good Human Life* (Cambridge: Cambridge University Press, 2010), 167.
140 Cousens and Mayell, *Depression-Free for Life*, 219.

CHAPTER NINE

Random Acts of Kindness

I have wept in the night
At my shortness of sight
That to others' needs made me blind,
But I never have yet
Had a twinge of regret
For being a little too kind.[141]

E ver watched the Christmas classic *It's a Wonderful Life*, staring Jimmy Stewart? In the movie the angel Clarence shows George Bailey (Jimmy Stewart) what his simple yet kind deeds had done for others and the tragedy that would have befallen their lives if he had never been born. It was Bailey's kindness that made all the difference in their lives.

In the hymnal "Have I Done any Good in the World Today?" are soul-searching questions: "Have I helped anyone in need? Have I cheered up the sad and made someone feel glad? Has anyone's burden been lighter today? Have the sick and the weary been helped on their way?"

---

141   Poem by C. R. Gibson.

Those questions are real, and there is no shortage of those in need. Thankfully there are good Samaritans everywhere looking for opportunities to brighten another's day. For some, it's being a gentleman—on a crowded bus, he stands so the elderly woman can sit down. It isn't that he has read Amy Vanderbilt's *The Complete Book of Etiquette*, but being courteous and kind just comes naturally to him. Or, as some say, "His mother taught him well." For others, volunteering at a soup kitchen or donating to Doctors Without Borders is more to their liking. For my father, the Scout motto "Do a Good Turn Daily" was his choice. It didn't matter if it was taking a friend to a Los Angeles Dodgers baseball game or buying shoes for a neighbor, it wasn't a good day until he had done something for someone besides himself. For my son John, it's not an unusual day to see him buying sandwiches and bottles of water to give to the homeless or using his legal training to defend those who cannot afford an attorney.

What will you do to brighten someone's day? It's your turn! It's an important step in saying goodbye to situational depression. Will you buy flowers for a widow, let the young mother with a baby go ahead of you in the grocery line, or write a check to the American Red Cross?

Whatever random act of kindness you choose, your day will be happier. Even two-year-olds are known to be "happier giving away Goldfish crackers from their own stash than from someone else's pile."[142] And here's a fact worth remembering: "random acts of kindness to those closest to you will make you the happiest."[143]

It won't take much to put a smile on your face if you decide to surprise your sister by doing her chores or put a sticky note on a mirror announcing that your brother's A on a calculus test

142   David Futrelle, "Can Money Buy Happiness?" *Time* (New York: Time Inc., 2017), 57.

143   Emma Seppala, "Secrets of a Happier Life," *Time* (New York: Time Inc., 2017), 20.

was amazing. How about flowers for your wife "just because," or what about a planned daddy-daughter date?

Years from now, you may not remember the thoughtful gesture of chores, sticky notes, or flowers, but in those acts of kindness you knew love. When love walks in as a result of your actions, there is little room for depression. Let me repeat that sentence in case you glossed over my words: *When love walks in as a result of your actions, there is little room for depression.*

If love walks in as a result of the actions of others, there is an element of sacrifice. The following personal story illustrates how the love/sacrifice connection will brighten your day.

With a Cadillac, a maid, and a gardener, my family always had a Christmas with the best gifts from Santa's sleigh. The days during which my parents struggled to survive the Great Depression were only whispers of yesteryear by the time I was born. Mink had replaced wool, and the country club societal whirl had captured my parents' fancy. In the 1950s they had become the American dream, and Christmas was merely an excuse to lavish each child with a fairyland of unrestrained wants.

My anticipation of opening gifts on Christmas Day was boundless, for I knew my mother was an uncontrolled shopper when it came to my whims. Being the only girl in a family of boys, I fared better than any at Christmas. My want list seemed to be surpassed only by my presents. After opening one gift after another, I toted my new acquisitions up and down the street so all the neighbors would know that Santa loved me best and that my parents were spoiling me to my complete satisfaction.

From such a worldly background of material prosperity, it seemed only natural for me to fantasize that when I had children of my own the established tradition of wealth and abundant giving at Christmas would continue—and that it would be even more lavish. If that had been the case, I would not have had one memorable Christmas—just more of the same.

Stuffed animals may have been bigger and clothes fancier and gadgets more sophisticated, but ho-hum can be found even in the abundant life.

It was in 1977 that my Christmas took a strange twist. Circumstances had changed. I was no longer the little girl awaiting the parental handout, but an adult attempting to make my own way in life. I was a graduate student in 1977, completing a doctoral degree and raising three small sons alone. Like several other graduate students, I had obtained university employment as a research writer for a professor; and like most of the students, I was struggling to meet my financial obligations.

Having more "month than money" had become my norm, but never more so than in December 1977. Five days before Christmas, I realized that my mismanagement of funds would prevent any ostentation in buying gifts for my children. In fact, it seemed to prevent much gift buying of any kind. It seemed unbearable to me—a young mother who knew all too well how to selfishly flaunt Christmas treasures before less fortunate neighbors, but not how to graciously be one of the less fortunate.

Cuddling my sons, I reluctantly explained the specter of our economic plight. My emotions surfaced as the children attempted to comfort me by nodding assuredly, "Don't worry! Santa Claus will give us gifts."

Cautiously I explained, "I think Santa is also having a bad year."

With certainty my firstborn son, Brian, announced, "But on television his sleigh is still filled with toys. With five days left till Christmas, he'll have plenty for us." His young brother Todd interjected, "Besides, Santa won't forget us. We've been good this year."

As all three nodded in agreement, I did too. My sons had been good. Yet, despite their goodness, they would soon be disappointed because neither Santa nor mother would bring the desired presents on Christmas Day.

That night I cried and pled with the Lord for relief, for a glimmer of hope that Christmas in our home would be better than I anticipated. My verbal prayers awakened my children. They seemed to intuitively know what was causing my unhappiness. "Don't worry about presents. It doesn't matter," said Brian. I knew that although it didn't matter on December 20th, it would be *all*-important on December 25th.

The next morning I could not hide the despair and self-pity that had marred my face through the night. "What is wrong?" I was asked again and again at the university. My trite reply was, "Nothing." Unconvinced friends pried and seemed in their own way to make matters worse. I snapped at the extended hand of friendship and grimaced at their undue interest in my personal life.

Arriving home, I methodically pulled the mail from the mailbox as I entered the house. A curious, unstamped envelope caught my attention. On the enveloped was typewritten, "To a very, very, very, very, very special lady." I gazed at the envelope and wondered if it were meant for me. Hoping it was, I tore it open. To my surprise I found several dollar bills inside, but not a note of explanation.

"Come quickly," I excitedly beckoned my children. Together we counted the money, examined the envelope, and expressed wonder at the anonymous gift. There was enough money in the envelope to buy an extra gift for each child. It was going to be a great Christmas Day after all. It wouldn't be as lavish as those of my childhood, but it would be good enough.

I was curious. Where had the money come from? Could it be from a neighbor, a friend, a classmate, or the bishop? Logical deduction led me first to near neighbors. Visiting from house to house in our neighborhood proved embarrassing. As I attempted to thank neighbors, each stammered and then confessed, "It wasn't me." Calling friends and thanking them elicited clever expressions. "If you find out who is giving away money, tell them to send some my way." Classmates rendered similar comments.

I decided it must have been the bishop. He knew what I paid in tithing and would be aware that a less than exciting Christmas would be awaiting my family. The children and I walked to his house and knocked on the door. Enthusiastically, we thanked him for his generosity. However, he denied being our benefactor and assured us that he did not know who had been so kind.

Curiosity mounted as nightfall approached. I read the envelope again: "To a very, very, very, very, very special lady." This time I noticed that the "e" and "i" were misshapen letters produced by an old typewriter ribbon. I observed that each dollar bill had been folded and unfolded many times, as if each one had been of infinite worth. My desire to discover the identity of the anonymous donor grew. Soon that desire was coupled with the gnawing resolve to return the money. The misshapen letters and folded dollars bills evidenced that the generous donor also had financial difficulties.

I couldn't sleep that night. Again and again I asked myself, "Who was it?" I had the clues of the old typewriter ribbon and the folded money, but not the answer. I can't really describe how I finally knew who the benefactor was, but about two o'clock in the morning, I knew. I knew who had a broken typewriter, and who needed to replace the ribbon, and who carefully folded and unfolded money, checking each dollar bill. It was my three sons.

With tears of love, I awoke the donors. Blurry-eyed they asked, "What's wrong?" I replied, "Nothing's wrong; everything is right! You gave me the money. You gave me all the money you possess!" Opening the bedroom closet door, I pulled out three empty jars that had once contained their treasured fortune. They were silent for several moments until my nine-year-old, Brian, turned to his younger brother Todd and punched him. "You told!" he exclaimed.

Attempting to fend off further blows, Todd yelled, "It wasn't me. It must have been John."

Their five-year-old brother immediately said, "It wasn't me," as both boys landed on him.

In unison they asked, "How did you know?"

I had searched outside my home for the answer—but the answer was within. I had seen generosity in all those around me, but had failed to recognize the generous hearts of my children. My house, with all its material flaws, was my heaven on earth, and my sons were my greatest treasure. Christmas 1977 was a merry Christmas worth remembering.[144]

It's your turn now—your turn to do a random act of kindness filled with sacrifice and love.

---

144 Story originally appeared in Susan Easton Black, "The Anonymous Bene-factor," in *Keeping Christmas: Stories from the Heart* (Salt Lake City, Deseret Book, 1996), 11-17.

CHAPTER TEN

The Courageous Choice

Although Cindy had shrunk much of the negative in her life and enjoyed surprising family and friends with random acts of kindness, she confided, "I still feel tired and depressed sometimes. Last night I tossed and turned most of the night. Some problems just won't go away. I feel mentally dull. Most days I take offense whenever possible."

It isn't time for Cindy or you to stop reading when depression still looms on the horizon. It is time to awaken your indomitable courage. The cowardly lion in *The Wizard of Oz* had the potential to be a king—he had the roar and the stature, but lacked courage. Wearing a simple shiny badge, the lion took on a new persona. He was resilient, confident, and courageous.

What does the lion have to do with you? Why do tornadoes happen in Kansas but not in Oregon? Why do hurricanes threaten beach communities in Florida and not in California? The answer is that the conditions are right, and so is the location— "the flatness of the land, temperature changes, humidity, and wind direction and speed."[145] Why did depression build a nest

---

145 Korb, *The Upward Spiral*, 12.

in your house? Conditions were right, but those conditions will no longer support depression when courage takes center stage.

A vignette from the life of Henry illustrates the seemingly immediate transition from depression to courage. Henry went from looking like a man who had sucked on a sour pickle for decades to an enthusiastic dreamer overnight. The transition began when he received a large Christmas bonus from his employer. The bonus, added to his savings, enabled Henry to put a down payment on a small beachfront property.

Henry envisioned himself surfing before and after work, hosting beach parties, collecting sea shells, and wearing Hawaiian shirts. To build a cottage on his property, Henry met with an architect, a contractor, and a banker. Then there were windows, kitchen cabinets, and bathroom fixtures to select. There was much to do and little time left for moping over past wrongs. He had to squeeze his dream in between work and family. To make his dream a reality, Henry needed to reclaim "free time"—time spent rehearsing negative thoughts.

Make Decisions

The first step in making your dream a reality is the courage to make a decision. Indecisiveness, the inability to make up your mind about relatively trivial matters, is a major symptom of depression.[146] By making a decision, you move out of the past and into the future. You move away from apprehension, hesitation, and reservation. Sound tempting? I hope so. As the old saying goes, "You gotta keep making decisions, even if they're wrong."[147]

You don't have to make the best decision—just decide. Are you stymied when buying a used car because the car doesn't

---

146 Donald F. Klein and Paul H. Wender, *Understanding Depression: A Complete Guide to its Diagnosis and Treatment* (Oxford: Oxford University Press, 2005), 27.

147 Korb, *The Upward Spiral*, 93.

have a dark blue exterior and black leather interior? If the car is within your budget, reliable, safe, and fuel efficient, buy the car. Are you paralyzed by wanting to fix the most amazing dinner with turkey, stuffing, candied yams, and homemade apple pie? Start by making a good dinner. Must you be the perfect parent? Start by being a good parent.[148] Focusing on the relative drawbacks of each option will make every decision less appealing.

Make a "To-Do List"

Like Henry, sometime in the morning during your shower or while brushing your teeth, you will do a mental run-through of your day—dry-cleaning to pick up, bills to pay, the carpet cleaner coming at two. You groan because it's Saturday—your free day. But no matter how many groans, you don't have the luxury of climbing back into bed either physically or mentally.

Perhaps you vowed to be at the fitness center by noon, make a potato salad for the neighborhood barbeque, or mow the lawn. Whatever your plan, while cleaning up after breakfast you will remember at least one more thing that must be done today. The reason is that goals—"have to do" and "it would be nice to do"—capture your attention from the time you wake up in the morning until you fall asleep at night. When you are depressed, most "to dos" are cast aside, but that's not the case anymore with Henry. He has a dream that exceeds his depression. He has to move forward through his day to free up spaces to fulfill that dream.

Is there an endless treadmill awaiting your day? I hope so. It's just what you need! When you were young, your parents orchestrated your time. In college, friends insisted, "You're not staying home tonight." But after that, the scaffolding for making the most of your day was taken away. Having a number of "to

---

148 Korb, *The Upward Spiral*, 40.

dos," social appointments, and daily routines is important to prevent a deep dive into depression. It is difficult to bask in the symptoms of depression when you know what your day looks like. Just knowing that you can't languish in bed affirms the all-important fact that you are needed.

It would be a "dull life" indeed if you eliminated the "to-do list." Having a list insists that you organize your day. Even one planned event in that day can make a significant difference in your mental outlook.[149] Give yourself strokes for washing and folding clothes, driving your son to his soccer practice, and balancing the checkbook. As anyone knows who has paid bills and discovers there is enough money in the checking account to cover expenditures, it is rewarding.

In speaking of those who accomplish such day-to-day tasks, President Theodore Roosevelt said, "Some sit on the sidelines, but the one in the arena is doing great things."[150] The great thing you achieved is a sense of accomplishment. Next comes freeing spaces in your day.

Consult the Calendar

It's time to get out that calendar—whether the calendar is on your phone or printed. Call me old-fashioned, but I like a sticky note on the refrigerator or bathroom mirror as a reminder. Whatever your system—make it work.

This day is going to be different. Tucked in between changing the sheets and turning in the overdue assignment is a journey into the house of tomorrow, and "the best thing about the future is it comes only one day at a time."[151] You may think that delaying "happiness in favor of getting more things done so that [you] can be even happier later" is the answer;

---

149   Fast and Preston, *Get It Done When You're Depressed*, 34.
150   Theodore Roosevelt Speeches, "The Man in the Arena," April 25, 1910.
151   Abraham Lincoln quote, in Aguirre, *Depression: Biographies of Disease*, 137.

not so.[152] You've been "playing it safe" long enough. What I'm trying to say is this: like the cowardly lion in *The Wizard of Oz*, move out of the routine—the "to-do list"—and add something extraordinary to your life. Put your dream on the calendar.

In the days of ancient Greece, courage meant bravery on the battlefield. For you, it is a simple notation on a calendar. To George, it was a reminder to ask the prettiest girl to the high school prom. To Kristen, a single parent with two daughters, it was a notation to enroll in a college course. To Jordan, it was a reminder to take the LSAT the third time.

Courage is the student who sticks it out in a difficult class, the mother who sacrifices for her children, the father who toils at a lackluster job for his family, and the football running back who endures pain and stays in the game. These are everyday people with everyday "to-do lists" who are willing to do something extraordinary against a background of seemingly impossible misfortunes.

For a moment, pause to dream with the *Man from LaMancha*, who explains in song his quest and philosophical underpinnings as he fights paper windmills and sees beauty in the wench Dorthea:

> To dream the impossible dream
> To fight the unbeatable foe
> To bear with unbearable sorrow
> To run where the brave dare not go
> To right the unrightable wrong
> To love pure and chaste from afar
> To try when your arms are to weary
> To reach the unreachable star.[153]

---

152 Seppala, "Secrets of a Happier Life," *Time* (New York: Time Inc., 2017), 12.
153 From the Broadway musical *Man from La Mancha*; lyrics by Joe Darian.

Order Your Priorities

Take charge of your life by taking charge of your time. There is no better place to start than ordering your priorities. Given the demands of the "to dos" of the day and the pervasiveness of technology, you inevitably face multiple professional and personal demands at once. For example, "you may be in a meeting at work but also watching for incoming texts from your spouse, who needs a ride home, or you may be finishing a work document while keeping an eye on emails so you can respond to a client right away."[154] Multitasking is a way of life. It is not unusual to see someone checking his phone at work, at the fitness center, on a vacation, or on a date. By multitasking, you can stay on top of day-to-day matters but unknowingly miss opportunities to brighten your future.

Guard your free time. Preserve your free time. It was famed Latter-day Saint artist Minerva Teichert who said, "I do not make calls or play bridge. That is the 'spare time' in which I glory."[155] The glory of her spare time was found in a paintbrush and palette.

Set Goals

The means to achieving a goal is not always obvious. For example, consider the millionaire who was asked to speak about how he achieved financial success. The convention center was packed with eager attendees hoping to learn how they, too, could become a millionaire. As the man stood up to speak, the crowd welcomed him with thunderous applause. The crowd listened intently as the man spoke of finding a pencil on the street and selling it for two pennies. He then said, "With the two pennies I was able to buy two more pencils. I sold those two pencils

---

154 Seppala, "Secrets of a Happier Life," *Time* (New York: Time Inc., 2017), 13.
155 Minerva Teichert to Professor B. F. Larsen, undated. Museum of Art at Brigham Young University Files, as quoted in Laurie Teichert Eastwood, *Letters of Minerva Teichert* (Provo, Utah: BYU Studies, 1998), x.

for four pennies." About five minutes later, he was telling the audience that he now had a hundred pennies. The man paused before saying, "My uncle died and left me a million dollars."

I am not ignorant of the fact that when you have been beaten down by life, you look at life through a darker pair of lenses and are more likely to accept lower expectations of yourself. Too often getting knocked down takes more than your wind. It takes your desire to get back up. I am not asking you to reach for the stars or win the Super Bowl, but I am suggesting that you set goals higher than washing the breakfast dishes.

How about taking that cooking class you wanted to enroll in last year or guitar lessons from the neighbor down the street? How about going on that vacation to Alaska or filling out an application for a different job? What about inviting a foster child to join your family or volunteering at a day-care center?

Although it was the philosopher Goethe who said, "Nothing is harder to bear than a series of good days," try it by reaching for your dream. Hollywood calls it *True Grit* starring John Wayne. Psychologists call it "alternative thinking." You may call it "goal setting." I call it "courage." It takes courage to set aside potential time instead of free time. Potential time is when you don't answer the phone or text messages, run errands, or fix dinner. It's your time to ponder, dream, and jot down a specific goal.

If there is a 100 percent chance that your goal will be realized, the outcome does not represent a goal. It is a certainty. Take, for example, an elderly woman whose daily goal is to get out of bed, walk over to the couch, and watch television. Her goal is easily met—barring physical limitation. Where is the challenge? Where is the courage?

Remember the childhood story—*The Little Engine That Could.*[156]

---

156 *The Little Engine That Could* by Watty Piper, pen name of Arnold Munk, owner and publisher of Mott and Munk.

The train cars were filled with toy animals, toy clowns, jackknives, puzzles, and books as well as delicious things to eat. However, the engine that was pulling the train over the mountain broke down. The story relates that a big passenger engine came by and was asked to pull the cars over the mountain, but he wouldn't condescend to pull the little train. Another engine came by, but he wouldn't stoop to help the little train over the mountain because he was a freight engine. An old engine came by, but he would not help because, he said, "I am so tired...I can not. I can not. I can not."

Then a little blue engine came down the track, and she was asked to pull the cars over the mountain to the children on the other side. The little engine responded, "I'm not very big.... They use me only for switching in the yard. I have never been over the mountain." But she was concerned about disappointing the children on the other side of the mountain if they didn't get all of the goodies in the cars. So she said, "I think I can. I think I can. I think I can." And she hooked herself to the little train. Puff, puff, chug, chug, went the Little Blue Engine. "I think I can—I think I can—I think I can—I think I can—I think I can—I think I can—I think I can." With this attitude, the little engine reached the top of the mountain and went down the other side, saying "I thought I could. I thought I could. I thought I could. I thought I could. I thought I could. I thought I could."[157]

Go out there! Take piano lessons, run a marathon, climb that mountain, then another—

> Climb every mountain
> Ford every stream

---

157 This version of *The Little Engine That Could* was told by President James E. Faust in "I Believe I Can, I Knew I Could," *Ensign*, November 2002.

Follow every rainbow
'Till you find your dream[158]

Be among the extraordinary people who know much of true grit, resilience, and greatness. That's what President Theodore Roosevelt did. "I am only an average man but, by George, I work harder at it," Roosevelt said. Don't fall in the trap of believing there is only one right way to reach your dream. Stumbling blocks arise even in the best-laid plan. Bad things happen, illness happens, and accidents, too, but the courageous press on.

At seventeen, Ettie Lee was a first-year teacher in a small pine-board schoolhouse in southwest Arizona. At Christmastime, it was expected that she would host a party for her students. Just as her party was getting underway, children rushed to tell her, "Miss Lee, Charles is outside." Charles was a young boy who had been expelled the year before.

"Tell him to come in," Ettie said.

At this, the wife of a school trustee loudly announced, "That boy has been expelled."

Ettie replied, "That was last year's mistake.... This is my party ... and it is my privilege to invite the boy." When Charles came through the door, the woman "grabbed the tea kettle from the stove and dashed the boiling water over the bewildered boy." Ettie turned to the woman and said, "I'm going to the trustees—I'll go to Phoenix—I'll go the governor if I have to. I'm going to get that boy back." And she did.[159]

Have the courage to make your dream a reality, and in so doing, I promise a ripple of hope will become a rushing current capable of sweeping down the mighty walls of depression.

---

158 "Climb Ev'ry Mountain" by Patricia Neway, made famous in the Rodgers and Hammerstein *Sound of Music*.

159 Ora Pate Stewart, *Tender Apples: A Biography of Ettie Lee* (Salt Lake City: Deseret Book, 1965), 177–179, 182.

CHAPTER ELEVEN

Hope

Randy and his bride, Melanie, stopped at an out-of-the-way Italian restaurant and ordered a pizza.

"The pizza is free if you correctly answer my question," the elderly restaurant owner said.

"I'll give it a try if you throw in a second pizza," Randy replied.

"Sure," said the grinning owner, "Here's the question. What's the greatest word in the world?"

Without hesitation Randy exclaimed, "Love."

"I knew much of love just like you," the restaurant owner said. "I had a wife and two children once. My wife and children were taken from me when bombs destroyed our village in World War II. My love was replaced by anguish and sorrow. Everything I cherished was gone. I thought all was lost until one dark night I looked to the heavens and saw the bright stars. In that moment, I knew all was not lost. I saw hope. *Hope* is the greatest word in the world."

The restaurant owner shared with Randy and Melanie the great secret for an abundant life. All of us will face disappointment and overwhelming sorrows as the years come and go. Love may be ripped from you and freedom from ailment may be gone forever, but hope always endures.

Daydreams, fables, and storybooks celebrate those who cling to hope in the worst of times. When adverse circumstances stamp out all possibilities, hope in legendary characters rises like a phoenix out of the ashes of despair. *Beauty and the Beast, Cinderella,* and the *Hunchback of Notre Dame* illustrate the truth that the unthinkable is possible if you have hope. Audiences worldwide applaud the literary geniuses of yesterday, for deep inside every soul, we all know hope holds our "hand when evening descends into night and when dawn appears to be too far away."[160]

The terminal cancer patient talks of cures, the penniless speak of mansions, and the farmer assures the banker that a bountiful harvest will cover his loans next year. Hope is college graduation, the allusive Prince Charming proposing, and a winning basketball season despite only a handful of victories. Ask anyone who has set an impossible goal and pressed forward against insurmountable odds—"Is hope in your equation?" Ask a mother if her wayward son will return to Church activity. If she is blinded by the reality of the moment, her answer is a tearful, "No." If she reaches inside to grasp hold of eternal hope, no stumbling blocks or looming boulders can mar her vision of what will certainly be. Defiantly, she replies, "Yes."

The downtrodden who allow situational depression to loom larger than life itself have lost the sure knowledge that hope is eternal. The downtrodden have learned by sorrowful experience to accept mere scraps, fragments, and crumbs of hope rather than a full banquet. They have forgotten how to paint in the rosiest tints a vivid vision of success and fortune on every front. They have forgotten how to pursue an ideal that may or may not prove illusory. Ask any victim of situational

---

160 Salman Akhtar and Mary Kay O'Neil, eds., *Hopelessness: Developmental, Cultural, and Clinical Realms* (London: Karnac, 2015), xvii.

depression if he or she too quickly abandoned hope and crushed the ideal. The answer will be a resounding, "Yes."

What the victims failed to realize is that hope can't be crushed. Hope is still there, for "no mirages of happiness or clouds of disappointment, nor the stupor of habit or the frivolity of thoughtlessness" can obscure hope. In other words, there is nothing so black that it can't be penetrated by hope—not even situational depression.

Recall the Greek myth in which the god Zeus unleashed vengeance upon Prometheus for stealing fire from the heavens. Although Zeus had every source of vengeance at his hand, he chose Pandora and her jar (now interpreted a box). When Pandora opened her box, a host of unspecified evils erupted forth upon an unsuspecting world. You name the calamity—whether sickness or death—Pandora was to blame. When she finally closed her box, there was only one emotion left inside. Long after passions were spent and sorrow was spilled recklessly upon a hapless world, it was hope that refused to leave the box.[161]

Such refusal of eternal hope is dissimilar in every way to such phrases as "I hope you'll feel better" and "I hope you get the job." The same could be said for phrases that punctuate newscasts: "There is hope the fire will be contained by nightfall" and "It is hoped that survivors will be found in the rubble." This type of hope is laced with doubt and uncertainty—the basis for fear and anxiety. It is this hope that philosopher Sophocles lamented when he said, "Hope is as a human foible that only serves to stretch out suffering." This damning view of hope places emphasis on hope being a fearful noun. "There's no hope for him," "That poor fellow hasn't a hope," and "There's little hope he'll ever make $100 a month more than his brother-in-law." In such usage, hope is defined as the chance or odds of the outcome may or may not be in your favor. It suggests

---

161   Hesiod, *Works and Days*. Translated by Hugh G. Evelyn-White (1914).

wishful thinking, which pointedly implies logic and thought pattern is faulty.

The hope the Italian restaurant owner knew much of is not the hope that Plato called the "foolish counselor" or Euripides claimed was the "curse upon humanity."[162] It is not what Francis Bacon called "a good breakfast, but a bad supper" or of which Benjamin Franklin warned, "He that lives upon hope will die fasting."[163] The hope the restaurant owner knew clung to him when he looked up to the heavens. This hope refused to leave him even in his darkest extremities. It sustained him when life's blows knocked him down.

Such hope is what climbing out of situational depression is all about. It is a hope that facilitates change, for it is present centered and future oriented. It is the hope that requires a future to play itself out. This type of hope has the ability to wait—to be patient—to believe that in spite of disappointment, you know all is not lost.

Martin Luther King Jr. had such hope. "I have a dream," he said. "Freedom must ring from every mountain side.... Yes, let it ring from the snow-capped Rockies of Colorado.... Let it ring from Stone Mountain of Georgia. Let it ring from Lookout Mountain of Tennessee. Let it ring from every mountain and hill of Alabama. From every mountain side, let freedom ring."[164] Anne Frank and Rosa Parks—everyday folks— had their hope, also. The famed boxer Muhammad Ali lit the torch at the 1996 Atlanta Olympics and demonstrated to the world that chronic illness could never snuff out his hope.

---

162 *The Polar Star of Entertainment and Popular Science, and Universal Repertorium of Great Literature* (London, 1830), 3:383; see also *Time: The Science of Childhood, Inside the Minds of our Younger Selves.*

163 Snyder, *Handbook of Hope*, 4; see also Cheryl Lavin, "Hope Is a Good Breakfast, but a ...," *Chicago Tribune*, July 9, 1995; "Misquotes and Memes: Did Ben Franklin Really Say," Baylor University, July 1, 2015.

164 Martin Luther King Jr., *Strength to Love*, 1977.

The hope that is lauded by humanity and literary greats alike is eternal and is the "dream of those who are awake."[165] After suffering the ravages of situational depression, you are now awake. You have been through a process of recovery that may have started with a family physician and may have included exercise, random acts of kindness, and goals. Whatever you chose to add to your life has brought relief. Any remaining vestiges of depression have moved off center stage, for the curtain has come down on the darkness of your life, and the custodian is sweeping up and ready to go home.

Deep inside you knew that depression would lose its grip. You also knew at some level that you were too important to stay in that dark cave any longer. You have weathered the storms of life punctuated with winters and springs "jumbled together in a puzzling array."[166] It could be said that you have weathered a storm of grand proportions and come out victorious.

I have seen the victorious leave therapy sessions confident that in a real sense their life is filled with a hopeful newness—a confidence that comes from knowing they are important. Although not a client, but in a real sense a client, such was the case with my husband Harvey. Rounds of chemotherapy, radiation, surgeries, and hospital stays affected more than his physical well-being. So much of what had made him an ideal husband was taken from him as he battled cancer year after year. I wondered if he would ever pull himself together after facing yet another disappointing medical procedure. When life seemed its darkest, Harvey reached for hope as if hope were the final straw—the essence of life.

Like Martin Luther King Jr., Harvey had a dream. It wasn't a dream for freedom or anything earthshaking to anyone else. It was a dream of taking a cruise to see the fall leaves on the eastern coast of the United States and Canada. With his physical

---

165 Joseph J. Godfrey, *A Philosophy of Human Hope* (Hingham, Massachusetts: Luwer Academic Publishers, 1987), 25.

166 Veninga, *A Gift of Hope*, 69.

condition, the dream seemed impossible and ill-advised to medical doctors, but Harvey was not to be deterred.

By the time he stepped off the plane at the JFK Airport and we took a cab to the New York Harbor Terminal, he was exhausted and longed for a bed. We moved through the check-in process rather rapidly, showing passports and credit cards. As I continued to matriculate through the check-in process, my husband found a seat and said, "I need to lay down. Can you get us on the ship right away?"

I checked with a crewmember to see how soon we could board. That was when I learned that only VIP (Very Important Persons) could board the ship immediately. The rest of the passengers, including me and my sick husband, needed to wait.

I found Harvey seated on a bench holding his head in his hands. He looked weak. I told him, "We can't board the ship now because we're not VIP."

"We *are* VIP," he said. "Go back and tell that man we are VIP."

I approached the crewmember again and said, "My husband and I are VIP."

He insisted on seeing my boarding ticket. "You are not VIP," he said. "You don't have a VIP boarding ticket."

I returned to my husband and explained the difficulty.

"Tell the man that you and your husband are children of God."

I paused. Although I had known since childhood that I was a child of God, I had never said it aloud except in song. Yet knowing the extreme suffering of my husband, I went back to the crewmember.

"It's you again," he said.

"It turns out my husband and I *are* VIP."

"Did you get a different ticket than the ticket you showed me?"

"No. But you need to know that my husband and I are children of God. How much more VIP can you get than that?"

Although he laughed, the crewmember shouted to his fellow workers on the ramp leading to the ship, "Make way for the children of God." As Harvey and I passed by a group of sailors, they bowed.

In spite of the mocking that day, my husband and I knew who we are and so do you. You are a VIP—a very important person. You are important by heritage and by what you have now accomplished. You haven't just fought paper windmills like the man from La Mancha, but you have fought a real and present difficulty that few can comprehend. You have fought situational depression and come out victorious. There may not be a referee holding your hand high and announcing your victory, but there should be. Secretly, I wish it was me.

As for our relationship, my dear reader and friend, we will probably not see each other until we meet in the celestial kingdom. They say the most surprising thing you'll see in the celestial kingdom will be the surprised look on other people's faces. I won't be surprised to see you, because you have learned how to overcome situational depression, one of the hardest trials of all. In your victory, don't be surprised when hope leads you straight to happiness. The happiness you'll find is an inward stability of blessedness—a confidence that life is worthwhile. It won't be 24/7 giddy happiness, and perhaps that's the best news.